FEEDIN`
B.I.T.C.H.E.S
COOK - DATE - RELATE

JASON ERIC LACISTE

ISBN: 978-1-967375-56-1 (Paperback)

ISBN: 978-1-967375-57-8 (Hardback)

ISBN: 978-1-967375-58-5 (E-book)

Library of Congress Control Number: 2025915691

Printed in the United States of America

Published by:

THE QUIPPY™ QUILL

info@thequippyquill.com
(302) 295-2278

WE'RE ALL HUNGRY,
WHY EAT ALONE?
WE'RE ALL THIRSTY,
WHY DRINK ALONE?
DON'T BE ALONE,
BE IN LOVE
OR LIKE, OR LUST...

ON THE INSIDE

INTRO

I consider myself an **average guy** who has experienced
GRATIFYing success in business, with WOMEN and with LOVE.
I AM TRULY HAPPY WITH LIFE, MY LIFE.
I can count all of my TRUEST friends on 10 fingers.
I told my mother I loved her every day until she died.
I have been **BLESSED**
To have traveled the world extensively.
And I believe that life is relationships:
Casual, Romantic, Spiritual.
WE CAN ONLY LOVE AS MUCH AS WE ARE LOVED.

I was engaged only once, and that was **THAT.**
I have never been, and I am yet to be married.
I've had the pleasure of meeting "a lot" of women
From around the world.
And though I've had few dates and even fewer
Relationships...
I've experienced every woman I truly ever wanted;
Body, **Mind and Soul.**

Today, I am experiencing like love and passion with
A woman who has always made me
want to be a better man.
I have always been and **I will always be a "hopeful" romantic.**

I LOVE FOOD, I LOVE FOOD, I LOVE FOOD.
AND I LOVE WINE, I LOVE WINE, I LOVE WINE.
BUT MOST OF ALL,
I LOVE WOMEN, BECAUSE THEY'RE ALL BITCHES....

B eautiful, bold, **BREAKABLE**

I ntelligent, **INTENSE**, independent, impulsive

T alented, tender, **TRUE**, trusting

C reative, courageous, **COMPLICATED**, cautious

H onorable, honest, **HEAVENLY**

E xquisite, entrancing, exceptional, **ELEGANT**

S ensitive, sweet, simple, **STRONG**, sensuous

Feedin' B.I.T.C.H.E.S. is a guide for men and WOMEN on **how to COOK, DATE and RELATE**. As well as REAL, **legit** COOKBOOK...! It is an UNDAUNTED collection **18 SUCCULENT recipes** AND OBSERVATIONS, reality and fact, of everyday people and how **WE** might APPROACH cooking and connecting to someone when **FOOD, WINE,** AND **SEX** (in the purest sense of the word) intersect.

The pages that follow are only a reflection of
MY **passion** for **food**, wine, and the **experience** it creates.
Words that may come off as "advice" are only from **MY experiences.**

As I said earlier,

LIFE IS RELATIONSHIPS. WE ARE ALONE WITHOUT EACH OTHER. SO LET US EAT, DRINK AND BE FULL TOGETHER.

WOMEN ARE

GUYS ARE

CRAZY, IDIOTS

FOR STARTERS

GET IT SET, GET IT CLEAN, GET IT STRAIGHT...

No matter how **BIG** or small, low rent or upscale,
the space that you inhabit is**... MINIMIZE.** Minimal is clean.
Get rid of it or hide all clutter, JUNK and mess.
CHUCK IT - under your bed, in the closet.
Just make sure she never finds it, smells IT...
Clean, scrub, dust, shine, sweep, vacuum...
All surfaces should be "sticky" free.

If she can't sit on it, she won't lay on it!

And the BATHROOM...
This is her last stop before meeting you in the "Promise Land",
So it better be immaculate, smell like roses...
Make sure the shower curtain is drawn, put a fresh roll out.
Check the bowl for **skid** marks, wipe down the seat, and close the lid.
A visibly nasty trash bin in the bathroom, **WILL NOT GET YOU LAID.**
Check your EGO.
Dating is HARD enough!
God knows how much nerve and wine it takes us all to date;
To ask, to say "yes"...
You've been CLUELESS for most of your dating life,
tonight BE NICE, or at least **AWARE-**
of who you are as a man, of who she is as a woman.

WHEN YOU FORGET TO BE A MAN,
YOU ACT LIKE A CHILD. AND YOU TREAT HER LIKE
A DUDE, OR LIKE THE GIRL IN 3RD GRADE YOU
USED TO HIT BECAUSE YOU LIKED HER.

Humility may not get you laid, at least on the first date,
but it will win you a smokin' hot new girl "friend"...of which you have few to
NONE.

And **BE** confident...
Confidence does not BRAG or BOAST nor does it call attention to what
YOU think you see in the mirror.
Save feeling ugly, fat and short for a night out with all of your other lonely buddies.

On this night, HER night and YOUR night as well...
LET HER SEE what she saw in you way before she said, "YES" to this date...
If you're new to dating, what worked 10 years ago definitely
DOES NOT work today.
And that means your clothes, shoes, cologne and your HAIR...

If you don't have a **CLUE**- ask a woman, any woman, your sister if you have to.
What women think goes a long way, "**all the way**" sometimes...

Scrub, clean, groom! ALL areas must be immaculate or sterilized if need be.
(And that goes for you B.I.T.C.H.E.S. too!)
Smelling fresh and clean is common sense- **MAKE THE EFFORT.**

If you can smell your cologne or your stink –

It's too much or you're still NASTY!

WASH AGAIN OR AT LEAST TAKE A WET WIPE TO YOUR UNDERCARRIAGE

(B.I.T.C.H.E.S. INCLUDED!)

Shave your face, trim and/or pluck your nose hairs.

UNI-BROWS and HAIRY BACKS, lord have mercy...

B.O. And BAD breath = Buh-bye, stinky...

There is no chance in hell of you gettin' the smallest "PIECE"

with dry lips and dry hands- MOISTURIZE!

And PLEEEEASE, NO AXE!! You're NOT 15.

No tight tees, no Under Armor, no Affliction T-shirts - they're not cool anymore...

Do I even need to mention Ed Hardy...?!

And Tommy Bahama screams, "Old Man"!

No Dockers, no Mossimo from Target...

No sweats, or any type of workout gear whatsoever.

No tennis, running, workout shoes - NO UGGS, NO River Shoes, TEVAS!

You're an adult, wear adult shoes.

And don't be afraid of brown leather or suede.

Her dad wears shiny black shoes...

And anything from ALDO or Skechers leave in your closet.

Make sure the socks match, no tube socks and no holes.

That nasty, smelly black crap under your toenails is shameful and a turnoff.

No bikini briefs, bikinis are for chics!

Calvin Klein undies are so Marky Mark, you're not Marky Mark.
Marky Mark even hates Marky Mark...
Black undies are always a safe bet, their slimming and hide all stains,
Not that there should be any...

A comfortable pair of jeans, not pegged, definitely not skinny and
an untucked white linen button down shirt can be sexy.

*The "skinny" on **skinny jeans**-
Nothing should bring attention to your **gut**, short and/or thick chubby legs-
Don't lie to yourself!
BUT if you can pull it off, **DO IT**- their actually pretty cool...

ON THE SIDE

WOMEN DO AT TIMES, GO "SIDEWAYS" BUT WE ARE JUST STRAIGHT UP DUMBASSES...

GET HERE INTO "IT", INTO YOU...

Music is a must...
And i can only offer two suggestions;
Save Led Zepplin for at least the 3rd date and
Miles davis, kind of Blue.
Too many words, too many riffs will get **IN** between you and her.
Kind of Blue is cool like, "Clooney"- **dare to be "Cool, Fool..."**
Music SETS THE TONE AND CREATES A MOOD.
Make sure she can **hear that mood** when she walks through your door.
The TV should be off, but if a game of SIGNIFICANCE is on,
Hit mute and turn the music up.

Bitches love champagne!!
VEUVE CLIQUOT not Korbell, could be a nice way to start off the evening...
Or perhaps, a fine tequila on the rocks or a nice scotch.
IT ALL DEPENDS ON HER...
KNOW WHO "HER" IS!

Stay away from the couch as long as you can.
A woman in a defensive position
shall not be kissed easily.

Standing in the kitchen is the easiest place to **get close to her**.
The music is playing, the wine is flowing, you're cooking like **Anthony Bourdain**
(when he used to cook...) and feeding her morsels of the greatest meal ever.

COMPLIMENT HER, something about her, whatever it is...
Examples-
What she's wearing, her shoes, hair, her mani/pedicure, her hands,
her fingers (as in, **long** and **slender**) Maybe she plays the piano...?
Just another way to compliment her, to get to know her, JACKASS...
HER EYES! Something, anything, ONE thing...!
Compliment her, it will give her a chance to compliment you.
But don't hold your breath. (Just giving you a heads up...)
Never talk about your eXes...
I made that mistake more than once, shameful!

Always listen and pause before you speak,

IF YOU REALLY HEARD WHAT SHE JUST SAID
WHAT YOU SAY NEXT WILL BE
EXACTLY WHAT SHE WANTS TO HEAR.

ALL WOMEN AT SOME POINT,
HAVE BEEN TREATED LIKE SHIT.
SOME ONLY KNOW SHIT.
AND A VERY UNFORTUNATE FEW
HAVE COME TO ACCEPT, SHIT.

So it is time that, **You – Johnny Romance**, show her the deal.
Show her for real, what it is to be treated like a lady...

BITCHES WANT ROMANCE!
And yes, romance is relative to who she is and who you are.

Women have needs. And that would be plural, as in many, as in —
You've got a lot of work to do.
BUT, fulfill those needzzzzzz and she will fulfill your NEED...!

Let me say again, WOMEN LOVED TO BE ROMANCED...!
And there are **countless** ways to ROMANCE a woman, give it sometime-
IT'LL COME TO YOU...!
But, if the **song is right** and the moment is there and **you can dance**
(buy a lesson, brother...!), then **DO IT** right there in the kitchen—
DANCE with her!
Place your hand gently on the SMALL of her BACK, pulling her close,
guiding and FOLLOWING HER at the same time.

Be close and hold her, but don't be a PERV.
Let her connect with you, connect with her - but don't be a PERV!

And even if you think she is giving you the sign to kiss her, DON'T!
The biggest mistake that guys make is ATTACKING when
all the woman was hoping for was a small advance, a **SLIGHT GESTURE**...

"LOVE" on her, not LOVE!
BUT SHOW HER HOW MUCH YOU REALLY APPRECIATE
THE THINGS YOU LIKE ABOUT HER.
Whatever you do next, will be **NATURAL** and appreciated by HER!

Just TRY...! The whole point of this book is, APPROACH.

Be different for a change! TRY a different approach!!!
Because to this point, whatever you have been doing or
NOT doing, HASN'T WORKED!

Only suggestions NOT directions: PICK some or at least ONE!
Take her hand in yours'. Hold it, caress it
As if you were holding something else of hers'...

Kiss her **softly** on the CHEEK, smell the nape of her NECK,
run your fingers through her HAIR...

BE SENSOUS and TENDER,
like a BITCH!

Again, for those of you who can't read-
DO NOT KISS HER at the first sign she gives you the "OK"...
it will make the actual first kiss, 100 times better
for her and for **you**.
And, YOU might BE WRONG-
MAYBE SHE REALLY DOESN'T WANT TO KISS YOU...

also, for crazies and dumbasses alike —
KISSING AND DANCING are good indicators of
"YOU KNOW WHAT..." WORK on that SHIT!

When **you're ready** and pray to god that **she** really **is**- GET IT...
But don't **RUSH**. Don't **EAT** her face, don't make her **GAG**.
Kiss her- don't sexually assault her...!!!!
No LOST or WANDERING tongues!
The tongue must have PURPOSE...!
Too much tongue could kill your cause...
And believe it or not, there are those out there that
DO NOT like THE TONGUE, so pay ATTENTION...!

*A small **disclaimer for my critics**-
Being into her, DOES NOT MEAN being A "girl".
Or as my friends **DOWN UNDER**, say, a POOFTA...!
YOU'RE A MAN THAT KNOWS HOW TO TREAT A WOMAN.
DO NOT fall into the "friend zone", being too sweet
Like the nerdy guy she could always talk to in
high school, but would never f*ck...

That being said, DON'T LOSE SIGHT OF YOUR OBJECTIVE-
CONNECT- CASUALLY, NATURALLY...
BUT, there may be times where you just have to take control.
Mid-conversation, go to her and
KISS her like she has never been kissed before but only for A MOMENT,
Just GIVING her a taste...

Sit back down and continue the conversation.
It's all about approach. But sometimes, the "animal" in us,
and hopefully in her, TAKEs OVER.

Finally, if by chance the date happens at her place and she has a pet or pets...
HER PET(S) were there long before you and they will be there long after you.
LOVE her pets or at least FAKE IT!
She will love or at least like you for one night.

THE MAIN EVENT...

EVENTUALLY WOMEN STOP BEING CRAZY,
IF ONLY FOR A MOMENT, BUT AS HARD AS WE
TRY, WE'RE STUPID, MOST OF THE TIME...

GET HERE. . .(not that way jackass!)

This night, this dinner, this moment whether you know it, realize it or
care to admit- is ALL ABOUT HER.

Nothing happens without her. So make it ALL about her **or**
be left alone with the hand...

BE interested in **her**, BE into Her- at least make it appear that way...
Attempt, YOU LAZY MF- to GET TO **KNOW HER,** GET TO **KNOW HER,** GET TO **KNOW HER**...!!!

If it were up to me, i'd stay in the kitchen, eating standing **up.**
Personally, feeding her bites here and there...
It's SEXY, SENSUAL and COMFORTABLE.

But, if you can offer a seat with a view, a sunset...
Something comfortable, not too formal that will ALLOW YOU TO BE A LIL' CLOSER to her than sitting
opposite each other at the dinner table, then do it- TRY...

Make sure she has everything she needs: sea salt, fresh ground pepper, water. Pelegrino is a nice touch.
Be sure there are napkins, not Kleen**EX**, on the table.

Be "CASUALLY ATTENTIVE". Casual keeps you cool and her comfortable. And a comfortable woman is easier to connect with, will allow you to connect to her.

Ask her about her- period! Not her "period" genius...
Women don't like to be told, especially random things about you...

ASK HER about her **passions, plans, likes** and dislikes.
Her middle name, her mom's name,
Know the answers to these questions if you want a see her again.

KEEP THE WINE FLOWING BUT NEVER POUR MORE THAN HALF A GLASS AT A TIME. ANYMORE, AND SHE'LL THINK YOU'RE TRYING TO GET HER DRUNK - EVEN THOUGH YOU ARE. ATTEMPT TO BE SUBTLE, STIFFLER!

And please, no Two Buck Chuck...
Do yourself a solid, go to Traders Joe's, there are amazing wines under $20.
GIVE HER A CHOICE: a light ROSE, a smooth WHITE, a bold RED
Will make you SEEM knowledgeable and educated in the FINER THINGS in **LIFE**.

Eat slowly. Eating fast makes you look sloppy and makes her feel RUSHED.
Chew with your mouth closed and don't chomp.
Let her taste and **enjoy your food** without any pressure...
And don't keep saying how good YOU THINK everything is...
If it's good, she'll tell you.

And you don't have to finish everything on your plate, this isn't mom's house.
You can have the leftovers after she leaves. overeating makes for a very
unsexy belly and potential gas.
so ease up, porky!
(And this could apply to the B.i.t.c.h.e.s.**, I'm just saying...)**

As hungry as you may be, never insist on finishing her food.
Maybe if she offers...but I wouldn't do it.

Again, don't rush through dinner, try to L**EARN** the most you can about her.
The more you know about her, the more she'll want to know about you.
But let her ask you–
Resist telling her HOW GREAT YOU ARE **for** once in your life...

Ask about her travels. Let her know about yours' or at the very least,
YOUR plans to travel.
SHE NEEDS TO KNOW, YOU KNOW THAT–

A WORLD EXISTS OFF OF YOUR COUCH, OUTSIDE OF YOUR APARTMENT, BEYOND YOUR ZIP CODE

TRAVELING - TRAVELERS ARE SEXY, EXOTIC ...

THE FINISH...!

IN THE END, WOMEN ARE STILL CRAZY, BUT WE LOVE THEM AND THAT'S THE ONE THING THAT MAKES US SMART, IF ONLY FOR 7 MINUTES...

GET ON WITH IT, IN IT ...

If at this point she is **STILL THERE,** YOU HAVE officially SUCCEEDED!
And at this point you better not be wasted!
Do not get too drunk! Maintain...**Giligan!**
It's about HER, make her feel like **no one has ever listened to her BEFORE YOU...**

IF YOU'RE DRUNK **YOU WON'T HEAR,
UNDERSTAND OR REMEMBER** ONE WORD **SHE SAYS.
HENCE, YOU WILL NOT BE GETTING LAID**!
NOT **THAT YOU COULD EVEN** GET IT UP
AFTER DRINKING **ALL** 3 **BOTTLES OF** WINE.

You can get drunk any other night of the week with your buddies,
Tonight you are with a woman, **ATTEMPT TO BE A MAN...**

DO NOT, I repeat DO NOT, attempt to give her a MASSAGE.
It's straight up creepy, let her come to you...
She will **SHOW YOU HOW** and **where** to TOUCH HER if you let her...

BUT...if you're going to massage anything, start with her feet,
NEVER going beyond the calves.
But it has to be GOOD!
If her feet ain't getting' it- **YOU AINT GETTING NONE!**

If she has had too much to drink, SUGGEST that she take your bed
while you stay on the couch.
Yo' bed best be clean, no DROOL on the pillows and
the sheets free of stains. Especially your own, Ewwwww!

And if by chance you are lucky enough to find yourself laying next to her
somewhere in your house, **RESIST,** RESIST, **RESIST**...!
KISS, **CARESS**, TOUCH every part of her body that she allows...
But don't be a PERV!

At this point if she is **STILL THERE, YOU HAVE SUCCEEDED**
far beyond your ridiculous expectations.
Remember, this night, this moment, this dinner - is ALL ABOUT HER.

UNBEKNOWNST TO THE MAJORITY OF MEN
WHO LACK COMMON SENSE, THERE ARE
WAYS TO **PLEASURE** A WOMAN WITHOUT
SUBJECTING HER TO **7MINS** OF
YOUR ROBOTIC JACK HAMMERING...

If you are uncertain...**ASK HER.**
If she can't or won't, or if she doesn't know what to say,
Then slowly find your way; kiss, caress and touch.
Guiding and following her at the same time-
And **ALWAYS** check in with her, making sure that she is still with you...

AND if at this point, she is **STILL THERE-**
YOU HAVE TO MAKE A CHOICE.
Because remember, WOMEN ARE CRAZY
and at this point in the night, or morning-
THEY WILL NOT MAKE THE CHOICE FOR YOU...

THEY HAVE COME THIS FAR...
And for whatever reason, they have found a PIECE of GOOD in you that
THEY HAVE COME TO TRUST...

AT THIS POINT, BECAUSE WE ARE MEN,
WE REVERT TO BEING COMPLETELY STUPID
AND-

WE, YOU- GO INTO ROBOTIC JACKHAMMER MODE AND COMPLETELY OBLITERATE

A PERFECT NIGHT THAT ONCE WAS!

This is IT or is it...?

SHE'S CRAZY, AND YOU'RE STUPID,
ESPECIALLY AT THIS POINT- GET IT!
MAY IT LAST FOREVER OR LONGER THAN
7 MINUTES...

GETTING IT!

HOLY SH*T, she's staying the night...or for about 7 minutes,
WHAT ARE YOU GOING TO DO ABOUT IT!

First and foremost, make sure there is water at your bedside
for the middle of the night, for when she wakes in the morning.
Give her the better side of the bed, the better pillow.
And let her know you're giving her the better side and the better pillow.

NATURE IS NATURE AND GUYS ARE GUYS,
so take this as you will...

As **Mr. Miyagi** said, "LOOK EYE, ALWAYS LOOK EYE..!"
(the aforementioned was a reference to the movie, The Karate Kid, **Duh**...!)
And I know you STILL don't get this, it means- **BE a MAN**!

While you are having **sex** with her, making love to her,
so laboriously **attempting** to **pleasure** her-

Take a peek into her beautiful eyes!
Just LOOK at HER, you Wuss!
Connect with HER!

YOU ARE NOT THE ONLY ONE THERE!
THE FIRST TIME, IS NOT YOUR PERSONAL
PORN SHOW!

It's about her, be into HER...
Women have ran from the gamet of PREMATURE men
who were only about taking the 7minutes to
satisfy themselves.
BE DIFFERENT, BE HER STUD...

And let me take a slight pause to talk about **"the MOVE"**,
and this goes out to you **B.I.T.C.H.E.S.** too!
Just because "the MOVE" worked in the past,
doesn't mean it will work with her!
We are **ALL** DIFFERENT. There is a **right time** and place for "the MOVE"...
There are **NO "sure things"** with BODIES that are all so different.

LISTEN TO HER BODY, HER RHYTHM.
there is more than **ONE** speed.
Even if it sounds like she is "READY"...

IN n' OUT might make for a good burger,
BUT IT WILL NOT SATISFY A B.I.T.C.H.!

Wait, be patient and witness her glory, still connecting with her gaze,
then FINISH IT, FINISH HER, but make sure
SHE FINISHES FIRST!
And bask in the GLORY TOGETHER.

If you do **IT** right this once, **WITH** her- who has so GRACIOUSly offered you a PERFECT piece of
herself,
YOU will reap
ORGASMIC pleasures
beyond YOUr most
PERVERTED dreams...

BUT NEVER FORGET,
IT STARTS AND ENDS WITH HER.
IF NOT, THEN WITH YOUR HAND!

You've Gotten IT,
SHE gave IT to YOU
or dare I say,
YOU earned IT...

NO MATTER HOW GREAT IT WAS, HOW GREAT YOU THOUGHT YOU WERE ... JUST SHUT UP AND SIMPLY TAKE HER HAND.

So IT was, what IT was...

HOPEFULLY THE TWO OF YOU GOT CRAZY
AND AREN'T FEELING TOO STUPID ABOUT
THE WHOLE THING...

GOTTA LOVE IT!

You may be laying **alone**, being that she left after you started **snoring**.
Or, you may be laying next to her- the both of you
too fearful to see each other naked **in the daylight.**

Or, she may be **orgasmically pleasuring you** under the sheets-
The STEAK ALWAYS does that to the B.I.T.C.H.E.S.!
Or, you may have learned something and
You might be under the sheets, **orgasmically pleasuring** her...

In any case, whatever happens next will be just fine if you
ALWAYS remember...

It's all about the B.I.T.C.H.E.S.
At their CRAZIEST, if you are **lucky**
enough to witness it and **smart** enough not to miss it...

THEY ARE PERFECT, PERFECT AND BEAUTIFUL. AND THAT IS WHY WE WILL ALWAYS BE IDIOTS- BECAUSE WE LOVE THEM; THEIR CRAZINESS, THEIR BEAUTY AND THEIR PERFECTION ...

WINE FOR my MEN before YOU RIDE!

I SHALL NOT INDULGE IN THE SPECIFICS
OF SPIRITS AT THIS TIME.
FOR I AM SAVING IT FOR
"DRUNK-ASS B.I.T.C.H." (COMING SOON)
BUT I WILL OFFER YOU THE BASICS...

BUBBLES

They all sparkle. A difference you can understand; region and price...

Cava - **Spain**, cheapest- I mean like less than $5 cheap...

Prosecco - **Italy**, just a tad more than Cava and somewhat on the sweeter side.

Champagne - **France**, the only bubbles that can be called Champagne.
On the higher end, depending on the year...

Sparkling Wine - CALIFORN-I-A...mainly **Napa**. From pennies to G's...

Suggestion not direction

Wine, like all things is relative. Relative to each person and
their very unique tastes. So, I'm only offering a guide-
FOLLOWING IS UP TO YOU.

Champagne can impress or even leave a LASTING IMPRESSION, so...

"If you really like her" - France, Champagne: Veuve Cliquot

"Kind of like her" - France, Champagne: Moet Chandon White Star

"You have no idea..."- All from Napa, all Sparkling wines: Domaine Carneros, Mumm, Schramsberg

"Don't ever want to see her again"- Napa, Sparkling wine: Korbell...

VINO as in wine...

Types and tastes...

Rose - not Blush or White Zinfidel, think of a white with a lil' body and color to it. Another approach to not drinking red.

Sauvignon Blanc - one of the lighter whites, good beginner wine, the new "white zin"...

Chardonnay - layers, flavors, "*oaky-butterness...*"

Pinot Noir - one of the lighter **reds**

Cabernet sauvignon - bold, with body, some **BIG**, some smooth like silk

All the wines listed above range anywhere from $3 to way too much...again don't be a tough-guy, ASK!

Suggestion not direction

Wine allows you to SHARE and TEACH - which could also make an **impression**...

Rose - **Marque De Carceres**, Spain, under $8 but pretty damn good...

Sauvignon Blanc - **Kenwood**, Sonoma, California. Basic, generic, but not cheesy. **Grgich Hills**, Napa, California. On the higher end, a lil' more complex in flavor. But if you gonna do this, you might as well spring for a bottle of chard...

Chardonnay - **Grand Ardeche**, France, under $7. For the price and the taste, I'll drink it all day...,**Sonoma Cutrer**- Napa, California. This is another wine with amazing flavor and still under $30 is definitely worth the price.

Pinot Noir - Some really amazing Pinot's out there from the Northwest, all pretty much in the same price range. **Acorbat** - Oregon and Cuvasion - Napa are both winners. Remember, Pinot's are on the lighter side, so they're **always a good place to start and end**...

Cabs - A good Cab will cost a lil'. A "decent" Cab will cost more than $10, so spend a lil' more. Only 2 suggestions;

B.R. Cohn Silver Label

under $15 but just as good as anything under $30.

B.R. Cohn Yellow Label

under $40 but just as good as...for the price and quality, I'll drink it all day and everyday...

To repeat, these were only suggestions of mine which I happen to LOVE. Ask, find out, seek what tastes good to you and your pocket - **wine tastings, another reason to drink and educate yourself!**

BEFORE you begin, Bitch!

AND THAT MEANS YOU, NOT HER!

GET THE ESSENTIALS

A real wine key, real wine glasses, silverware and dishes- **ALL CLEAN.**
Get most of the prep work out of the way; washing, cleaning, cutting, dicing.
It should all be organized and ready to go, so it appears
you know what you're doing...
But, save a lil' to show her; some dicing, washing of the lettuce,
crumbling the Bleu cheese...
YOU STANDING THERE WITH YOUR LONG KNIFE, TOWEL DRAPED OVER
YOUR SHOULDER "DICING", IS HOT.!

Methods, Metals, Meanings and Measures

The PURCHASE

In order to become a cook, a decent cook or an even better cook-
YOU HAVE TO STOP SHOPPING AT MARKETS THAT HAVE "**club cards**".
Better, **high-quality ingredients**, specialty items that are unique, from across the
pond, from afar off places you have never heard of, make for a better meal.
Make you look better – give you something to talk about.

At Albertsons, "prime" is just a sticker slapped on a **random piece of meat**
And "fresh" means **thawed...Make an effort** , **son!** At the very least, Pavillions...

Solid bets; Wholefoods, Trader Joe's, BRISTOL Farms, your local Farmers Markets or butcher.

Your CHOPS

if all the knives you own are **serrated, look like a saw**, and/or have the letters
I-K-E-A printed on them, SHAMEFUL!
YOU'RE A MAN, YOU NEED A REAL KNIFE-

Something **long**, sharp with some weight to it.
And it MUST be sharp. An adequate, sharp knife cuts with ease.
We are not all created equal, but you can buy a big knife…

The METAL

You need only 3
A sauté pan, simple rule- the heavier it is, the better.
A medium sized sauce pan, like your sauté pan but with sides and a lid.
Last, something BIG- for pasta, for sauce, for boiling lots of water…

The CUT

The CUT of everything you **prepare, cook** and serve is crucial.
Everything she puts in her mouth should feel good
(PERV!) and the cut makes all the difference!

chop: cutting food into small, bite-sized pieces
dice: to cut food into very small pieces, diced food is smaller than chopped food.
slice: cut it thin, LONG ways…
Mince: to cut food into tiny "cubes", just smash it and chop the sh*t out of it…
Julienne: cut into long strips, like "shoe strings". Length and thickness varies, usually smaller, fine slices.

My MEASURES

"Turns"; as in your pepper grinder, hopefully you have one.
If not, shell out $3.99 for the see-thru plastic one at the market.
Real pepper makes for **REAL FOOD**…
"Pinches"; as in seasoning. "Nice" pinch- 3 fingers,
"Generous" pinch- 5 fingers.
And let this apply to food ONLY..

"Counts" – as it refers to "dressings", I'm speaking of oils and vinegars; As is in, olive and balsamic.

Flip the bottle let it flow and count, "1 count" – count to 1 or 1 "Mississippi" or 1:1000, get my drift. A "4 count" would be...

"Shots" and "Splashes" – apply to both seasoning or dressings, amounting to a single "count" with some "**bass**" to it. As in a beat, not a fish...

As in, more fingers, a bigger pinch...!

The WASH

Anything green, any veg, and especially fresh herbs should be cleansed of anything brown- That would be dirt.

NOW it's time to cook, BITCH – yeah YOU!

ALWAYS REMEMBER...
WOMEN ARE CRAZY BITCHES...
YOU, ARE AN IDIOT!

THE STARTERS

Roasted PISTACHIOS in the shell

Mother of ALL- SHRIMP Ceviche

"Local" style AHI Poke

European Cutting Board with TRUFFLE Honey

Steamed Sweet CLAMS and Spicy Andouille SAUSAGE

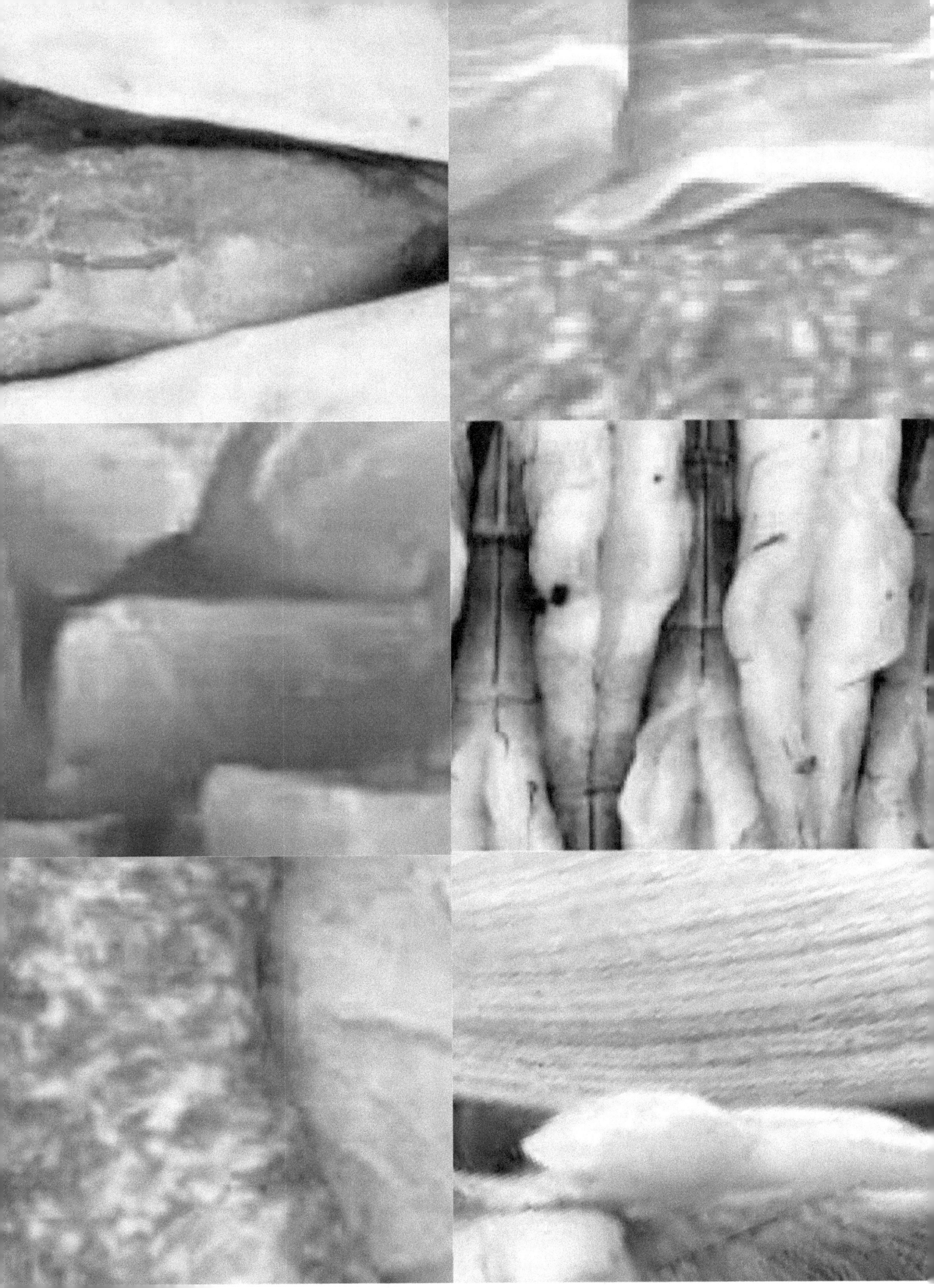

BELIEVE YOU ME, IF A WOMAN IS COMING OVER, THERE'S ALWAYS A BOTTLE OF WINE AND SOME NUTS WAITING FOR HER...

Roasted Pistachios in the shell

If you're not a pistachio guy, peanuts will do. In the shell, of course... The whole point of the NUT is, it gives you something to do. Your hands, her hands, cracking- BUSTING NUTS. We always speak easier when we're doing something. it's finger food and with that, a chance to feed her, for her to feed you- **GETTING YOU ONE STEP CLOSER TO "INTIMACY", PERHAPS...**

INGREDIENTS

1 bag of Roasted Pistachios,
    "salted" equals swollen fingers and
    dry lips, but it's up to you...

DIRECTIONS

You'll need 2 bowls.
NOT your cereal bowls. Nothing too big
And hopefully matching.
Put your nuts in 1, the other empty for shells...
It's that SIMPLE **Emeril...**

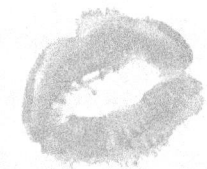

Mother of ALL – Shrimp Ceviche

Just so you know, and in case she asks, ceviche is from South America, not **Mexico**. (With the "Mother of all Ceviches" coming from Peru, I have heard...) It's not "cooked" as we know "cooking" to be...but SEARED in the juice of limes you **squeeze** FRESH by hand...**For the record, NO "trendy" restaurant in la serves ceviche the right way! Always** F*CKING **it up by adding fruit and a big price tag to it...**

INGREDIENTS

1 lb Shrimp
> Small to medium deveined fresh, **NOT frozen**

1 small Red Onion

1 large Jalapeno Pepper

7 Limes
> Save at least 2 halves of lime, you'll see why later

1 bunch of Cilantro

Sea salt

DIRECTIONS

Cleansing your cilantro-
Take one of your cereal bowls, fill with water and dunk cilantro, leaves side in... swirl a bit, shaking loose any critters or "earth" that may be hiding. Then let it rest on a paper towel.

Roast your Pepper
Turn your burner on high, put your pepper in the flame resting it on the racks of the burner...it will crackle and pop, **but let it be until** black. Then turn it, til' the other side be black. When your pepper BE black, set aside and let cool.
Thinly slice your onion.
Juice 7 limes, loosely chop cilantro.
Dice the sh*t out of your roasted jalapeno.
In a large glass dish or bowl mix-

Onion, jalapenos, lime juice. Slice your fresh, DEVEINED, shrimp lengthwise creating 2 equal halves, toss with onions, jalapenos and lime juice. The lime juice does make it tart, so add salt to BALANCE THE FLAVORS, but don't over salt! ENHANCE, don't overPOWER the fresh flavors of the shrimp and lime. Cover and chill in refrigerator for at least 45mins. Generously garnish with cilantro before serving.

*As for the 2 halves of lime that you saved, before taking that already NASTY sponge that you use for dishes to your now "shwimpy", slimming cutting board- use each half and scrub down your board. This pre-cleans it and gets rid of that "smell". It will also prevent you from contaminating anything you cut on your board thereafter.

But you still have to take a sponge and dish soap to it, Martha...!

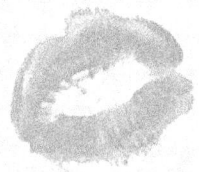

"Local" style Ahi POKE

By "local", I mean born and raised HA-waiian! And it's pronounced "Pok-EH" not POKE...roughly translated – cut piece or small pieces

INGREDIENTS

1lb. FRESH Ahi, Aka- Yellowfin Tuna.
    Steaks or blocks...
    And IT MUST be fresh, SUSHI GRADE!
    Spend the cash or
    WORSHIP THE BOWL!
1 medium Sweet White Onion
1 bunch Green Onion or Scallions,
    Spring Onion (they're all the same)
Toasted Sesame Oil, 4-6 tbsps
Chili flakes
Coarse Sea Salt

DIRECTIONS

Cut fresh Ahi into bite sized cubed pieces-POKE! Thinly slice your onion, finely chop your green onion.

In a large bowl combine; fresh Ahi, white and green onion, 1-2 pinches of chili flake. How much heat is your call but try to GIVE IT SOME KICK! Give it 2 generous pinches of salt and a nice drizz of sesame oil. 4-6 tbsps usually does the trick. Your poke should be moist and succulent, not dry. Mix all ingredients, gently but completely. Cover and refrigerate at least 20 minutes before serving.

A light cracker might be a nice touch to your poke. Giving you yet another opportunity to offer up some of your finger food, hand to mouth. Another step closer to her lips...

One last thing, **don't add** avocado **to MY poke, it ain't tuna tartar...!**

European Cutting Board with Truffle Honey

You have nothing to do with the preparation of the ingredients, so there should be NO WAY OF SREWING THIS UP. It's all in the presentation...

INGREDIENTS

Decent sized Cutting board
> Hence the name...
> **(make sure it's like your sheets–
> CLEAN and NO STAINS!)**

At least 2 premium Cured Meats
> 8-10 slices of each is a good measure
> Serrano Ham and Genoa Salami are
> always good bets...

3 premiums Cheeses
> My "go-to's" SAINT Andre, Manchego,
> Burrata. When in doubt, ASK, the deli
> guy!

Truffle honey
> Truffles are basically mushrooms,
> fungus (but don't ever call'em that...!)
> that cost $2000 per round.
> Pricey but...make EVERYTHING
> taste, UNbelievabe...!

Rasberries or Blackberries
> 1 basket

DIRECTIONS

Arrange meats and cheeses on cutting board, try to **be creative**!

As with yourself, presentation is a huge part of this dish. MEAT, CHEESE, BERRIES – "PAINT" something...!

And **CUT the cheese**! Some of it at least...Think, deck of cards fanned out on a blackjack table. (Not sure if that helped, just trying to help you visualize.)

VARIETY is a must and CONTRAST is cool. That means each meat and cheese you choose, is DIFFERENT...

Know what you bought and the difference between each.

This will "maintain" the illusion that YOU know you're doing...

A light cracker is a nice option to give her. **AVOID the baguette**, no reason to fill up on bread.

I like to DRIZZLE the honey on the board somewhere amidst the **salty** and CREAMY **goodness**.

But if you have a small enough side dish, that'll do...

And again, you are presented with another finger food and the opportunity to...

The truffle honey is the **BEST** and **SEXIEST** part of this dish.

A rich morsel of cheese DIPPED into the SWEET honey, with the perfect SALTINESS of the Serrano Ham, makes for the **perfect mouthful**...

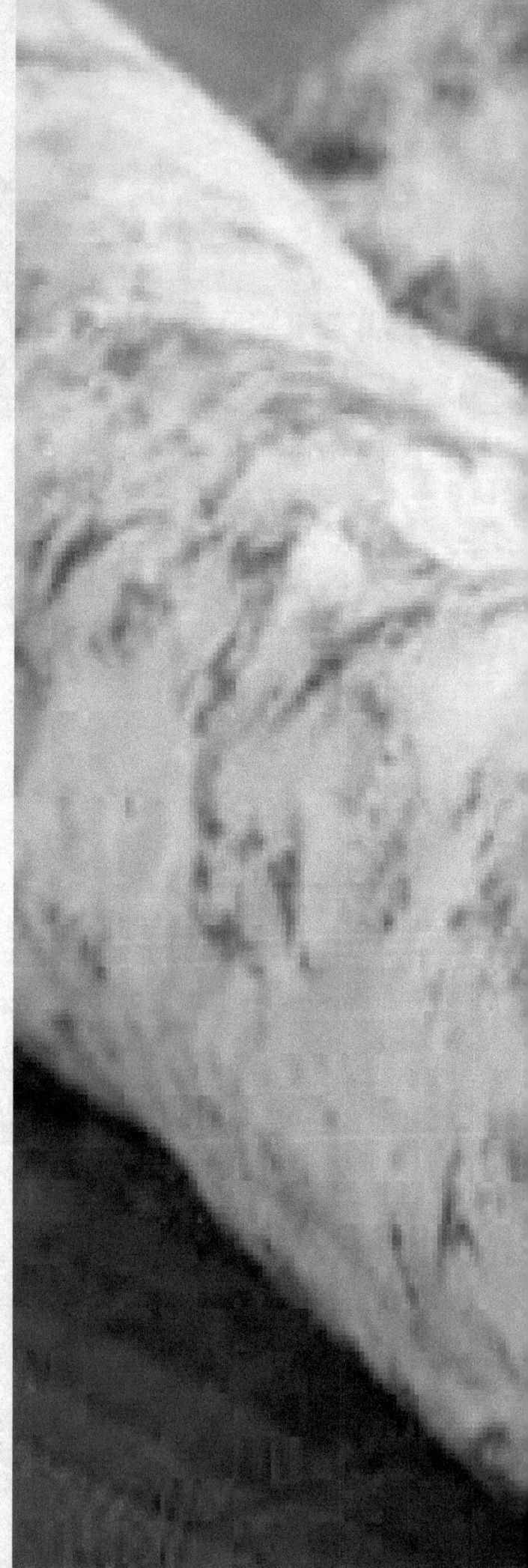

Steamed Sweet Clams with Andouille Sausage

It sounds complicated but it's not; big pot, a lil' water, throw the stuff in it, cover and let it steam...

INGREDIENTS

16 Manila Clams
    (10 is too little, 20 too much)
2 gourmet Andouille sausages,
    No Jimmy Dean's, Hillshire Farms
6 cloves Garlic
1 large White Onion
1 bunch Parsley
1 generous cup **drinkable** White Wine
½ stick Butter
Sea salt and fresh ground pepper
Lemon

DIRECTIONS

With a kitchen brush or scouring pad, scrub your clams.

They should be clean, sealed tight and not smelly.

HEAT large sauce pan (that has a matching cover) over high heat, hitting it with a nice splash of olive oil. Thinly slice onion, smash-mince garlic and add to pan, adjusting heat to medium.

Saute for 3-5 minutes. Add a generous cup of drinkable white wine, cover and let the JUICES "**MARRY**" for a few minutes.

At this point, fire up the grill and cook your **sausages**. **I believe** you can do more than one thing at a time.

Back to your pot, let the clams join the party. With the heat still at medium, cover and let simmer.

You will NOT let her **eat rubber**, so you will NOT overcook your clams. Keep an eye on them, popping the lid and checking on them.

As they open, with a bowl ready at the side of the pan, place the popped clams in the bowl. Replacing the lid on the pan allowing the other clamies to open in their own time.

The reason gents, this will prevent the "rubbery" clam.

Don't forget about your sausages, if you can't grill a sausage, SHAMEFUL....

When all the clams have opened for business, and you are left with only the "**Jus de clam**", turn the heat up to high and add your half stick of butter. By now your sausages are ready, slice and set aside. As the butter melts turn off the burner.

1 generous pinch of salt will suffice and as will 3 turns of pepper. Serve the clams in bowls, 8 for you, 8 for her...

Bath each bowl with the **beautiful broth** that you have just created, top the lil' Clamies with your grilled Andouille sausage and loosely chopped (WASHED) parsley leaves and **VIO**LA..!

NEVER FORGET... WOMEN DO AT TIMES,
GO "SIDEWAYS" BUT WE ARE JUST
STRAIGHT UP DUMBASSESS...

THE SIDES

Grilled ROMAINE Salad
with Sweet & Spicy PECANS and BLEU cheese crumbles

CILANTRO Lime Slaw
with Asian PEAR and Roasted JALAPENOS

"Not your Mama's B.S." – that's Brussels SPROUTS
Roasted with Crispy PANCETTA Flakes

Grilled sprouts ASPARAGUS - Straight Up Son!

Maui Macaroni POTATO and EGG Salad

Grilled Romaine Salad

with Sweet & Spicy Pecans and Bleu Cheese Crumbles

Yes, "grill" the lettuce. its sounds weird because you've never tried it, INexperience is UNinteresting. Like anything you grill, it just makes it taste better.

INGREDIENTS

2 Hearts of Romaine lettuce

Sweet & Spicy Pecans, nice handful

> TJ's, WH's, both carry candied, spicy and/or Sweet & Spicy Pecans. I could offer a recipe but that would just be too much work.

Bleu cheese

Extra Virgin Olive Oil

> (pay the extra $5 Mr. Furley, good olive oil makes everything taste better!)

Balsamic Vinegar (same as olive oil...)

Sea salt and fresh ground pepper.

DIRECTIONS

Heat grill on high heat.

Give your romaine a nice cleansing down to the butt/root, ridding your greens of any critters or "stuff". Cut each heart in half, **don't cut off the "butt"** or root of the heart, this will keep the leaves of the lettuce together on the grill.

But remember, once on the plate, don't eat the butt…all the way down to the butt, but not the butt, **unless you're that kind of guy...**

Generously drizzle each heart with olive oil, 2 generous pinches of salt and 2 turns of pepper.

Turn grill down to medium heat and place hearts face down for just, 1-2minutes MAX.

Because of the oil, your grill will FLARE UP. But this only adds to the taste and presentation of your "grilled" salad. Remove from grill and plate.

Remember, presentation adds to the experience of how food tastes, be creative with halved HEARTs...

Paint, "build"...EXPRESS!

Drizzle with olive oil, splash with balsamic vinegar and give it 1 more turn of ground pepper.

Finish with crumbled bleu cheese and crumbled sweet/spicy pecans. That means YOU crush, smash, crumble the cheese and NUTS-

USE YOUR MANLY HANDS, MAN!

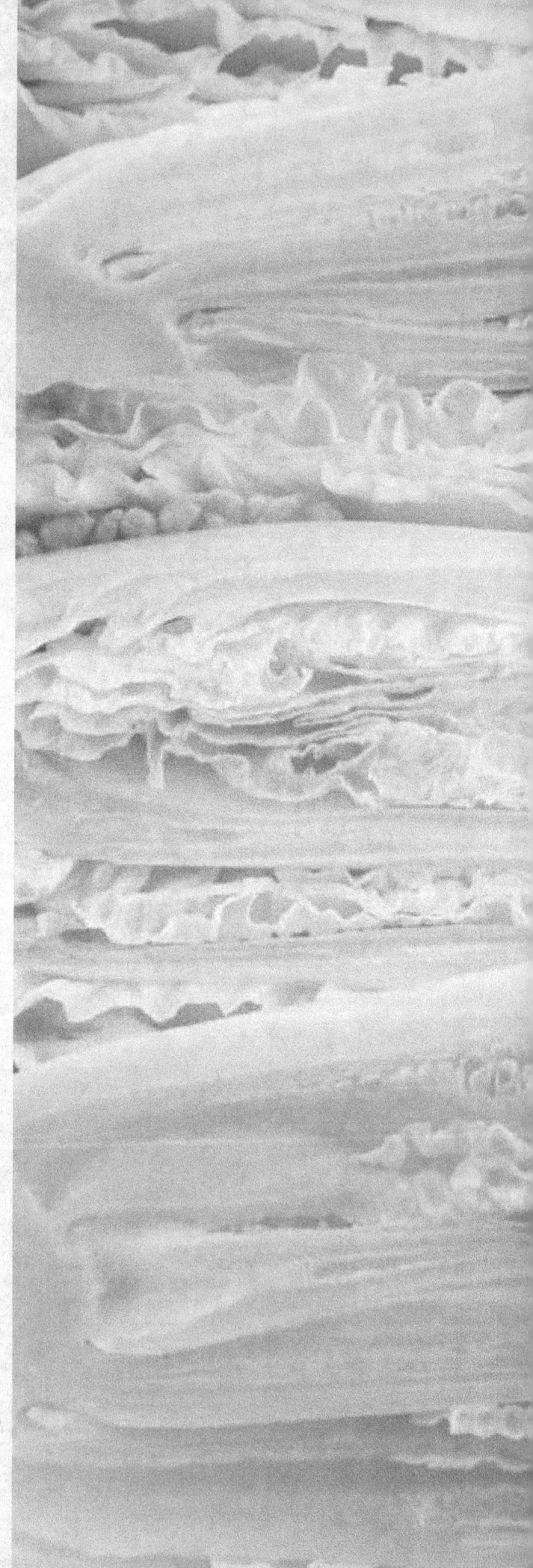

CILANTRO LIME SLAW WITH ASIAN PEAR AND ROASTED JALAPENOS

Just a note: this is a really light salad that is meant to go perfectly with seafood. And for those who think CILANTRO tastes like **soap**, you're insane and what the hell are you doin' eatin' soap...?!?!?!.

INGREDIENTS

2 bunch Cilantro
> Pick a good one, fresh herbs should look more green than brown...

1 Small red onion

1 Asian pear

1 large Jalapeno pepper

1 Avocado
> RIPE, "Al dente". Firm but nor too soft...

3 Fresh limes

Sea salt and fresh ground pepper

DIRECTIONS

Get the "wash" on your cilantro and set aside on a paper towel to drain.
Roast your Jalapeno.

The CUT
Everything she puts in her mouth should feel good (**PERV!**),
so the CUT makes all the difference!

Thinly slice onion, JULIENNE pear, dice avocado, and chop cilantro. Remove stem and seeds from jalapeno, finely dice.

Lightly toss all ingredients, saving the avocado for last. You're not making guacamole (at least, not yet). NOW, mix but don't mash the avocados!

This slaw though light, packs a lot of flavor.

Only salt and pepper as needed...

"NOT YOUR MAMA'S B.S."

THAT BE BRUSSELS SPROUTS, ROASTED WITH CRISPY PANCETTA FLAKES!

This dish is a no-brainer. if you can't pull it off, I've got NO sympathy for you...

Yes, none of us liked'em as a kid. But you're a man now, tater tots are NOT veggies!

INGREDIENTS

1 lb. Brussels sprouts

You can get them off the stalk or bagged at most markets.

Pancetta

4-6 slices from the deli. It's Italian bacon, but PLEASE don't use bacon. You eat bacon all the time, **B.i.t.c.h.e.s deserve pancetta...**

Red Wine Vinegar

(NO, it's not the same as balsamic...!)

Extra VIRGIN Olive Oil

Sea salt and fresh ground pepper

DIRECTIONS

Preheat oven to 425 degrees F.

Cut Brussels in half.

In a large bowl, toss halved Brussels with a "3 count" of olive oil, 2 generous pinches of sea salt and 4 turns of the pepper grinder.

Spread evenly onto a cooking sheet and roast in the oven.

While the Brussels are ROASTing, heat a frying pan on high heat. After 3-5 minutes, or when your pan starts to smoke, add your pancetta to the pan and reduce the heat to medium-high.

After 20 minutes, it's a good idea to give your Brussels a **turn and a toss** for even cooking. Return to the oven and continue roasting for another 15-20 minutes.

Back to your pancetta, as I said earlier- it's Italian bacon, **you know how to cook bacon.**

You want a nice crispy caramel brown, don't burn it! 3-4 minutes on one side, 2-3 minutes on the other side should be safe.

When perfectly crispy, set on a paper towel to drain excess oil.

At this point, your" B.S." should be ready. When your Brussels are done, they'll have **a nice "char", a lil' crisp and some brown to them.**

A serving platter or larger than normal plate would be the way to serve your sprouts.

Crumble your crispy pancetta over the top of the sprouts, give them a nice splash of red wine vinegar and a drizz of olive oil and you are done, **Johnny Romance!!**

GRILLED ASPARAGUS – Straight up, SON!

Yes, it does make your pee stink, but it's an **adult** veggie. It's **sophisticated** and easy, **Johnny Utah** (not the same as Johnny Romance...!

INGREDIENTS

1 bunch Asparagus
Extra Virgin Olive Oil
Balsamic Vinegar
Shaved Parmesan cheese
Sea salt and fresh ground pepper

DIRECTIONS

Fire up the grill on high.

Trim the Butts of the asparagus. They should be green from tip to butt, any brown around the butt, chop it off...!

Toss asparagus generously in olive oil, a splash or 2 will do, 2 pinches of salt and 2 turns of pepper.

Reduce heat to med-high and grill your asparagus 8-10 minutes, giving them a roll after 5 minutes for even cooking.

Your spears should be **somewhat firm, DEFINITELY not** limp, and have a nice char.

Plate your asparagus, giving them a splash of both olive oil and balsamic vinegar.

Finish with a 5-finger pinch of shaved parmesan.

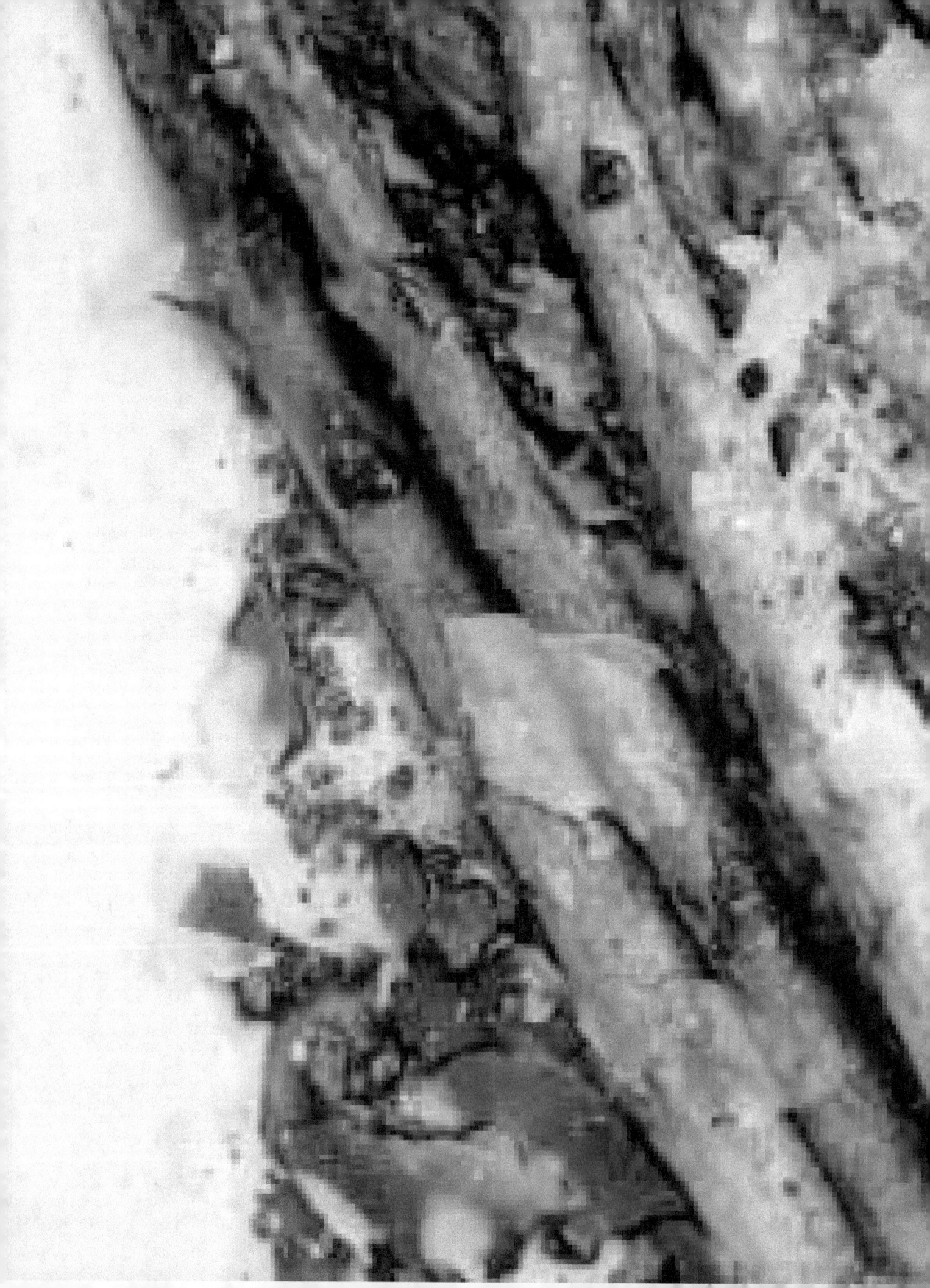

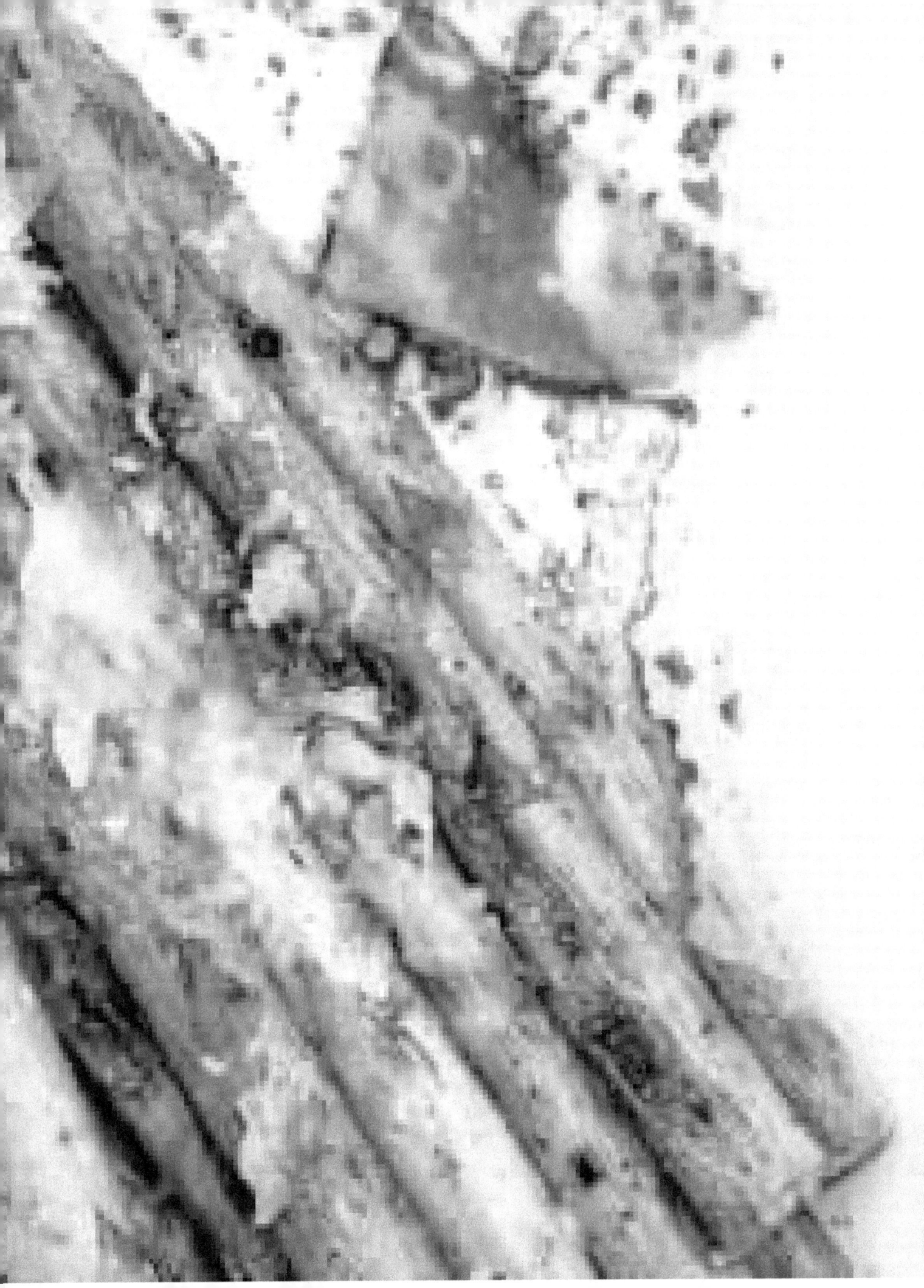

MAUI MACARON POTATO and EGG SALAD

Now, where I'm from, "Mac Salad" doesn't scream gourmet. But it seems that **women love mayonnaise**, I'm just saying...

INGREDIENTS

1 bag/box Elbow Macaroni Pasta

4 Red Potatoes

4 hard-boiled Eggs

1 small Red Onion

1 bunch Green Onion

1 medium Carrot

1/2 10oz bag Frozen Peas
        thawed and drained

Mayo, 1- 1 1/2 cup

Sea salt and fresh ground pepper

Paprika

DIRECTIONS

In your large pot, fill 2/3 with water and heat to boil.

Your eggs should/could be done ahead of time but if not...Cube red potatoes, drop your eggs and potatoes in the boiling water.

Here you're saving time, killing two birds with one pot...of boiling water. **You're cooking, dare I say, like a chef**...

Remove your eggs after 9 minutes and give them an ice bath. Let your "pots" cook for another 4 minutes or until you can **stab** them easily with a fork. When your "pots" are done, remove and set aside to cool.

With your water still going, which might need a refill, add a cup or two, and bring it back to boil. Throw in 2 generous pinches of salt and a "2 count" of olive oil and add your macaroni.

One word here- "**AL DENTE**"! Italian for "firm to the tooth..." or for you - firm but not soft in the mouth. All it means is, **don't overcook your pasta**! it'll give your dish texture instead of tasting like a big bowl of mayonnaise mush...

While cooking, give your mac a couple of stirs so you don't end up with one big ball of MAC. 8-12 minutes, max cooking time.

Remove from the pot, strain, and bath with cold water. Set aside to cool and drain.

The "CUT" of everything you cook and serve is so **crucial**, but in this case we're going to make it easy for you...**CHEESE GRATER**! Using the largest cut on your grater, grate your skinned and halved onion and carrot into a large bowl. Your eggs can also be grated or finely chopped.

Add your cooled mac, eggs and pots to the mix, along with your peas, mayo, 2 generous pinches of sea salt and 6 turns of the pepper grinder.

Toss lightly, mixing mayo throughout. There are a lot of flavors going on in this dish, so don't drown it in mayo...

Finely chop 2 stalks of green onion, use to garnish the top of your mac. Hit it with a couple of shots of paprika for some color and another layer of flavor, and you are done!

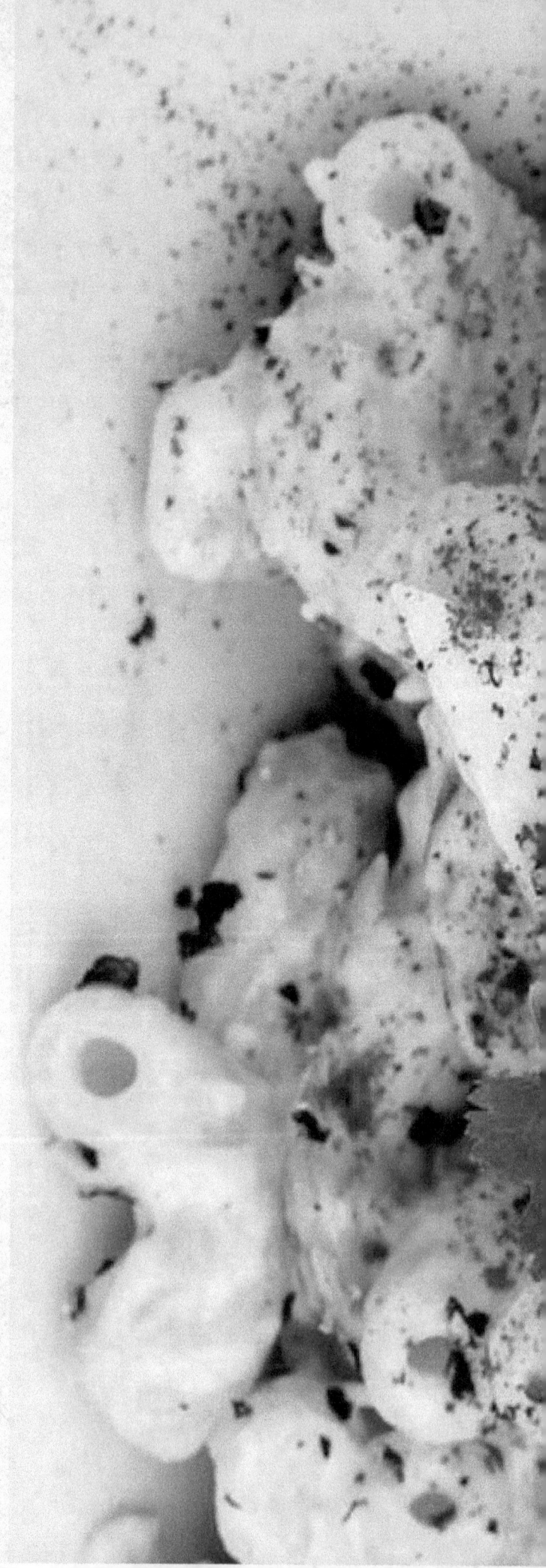

IT'S TIME COOK YOUR ASS OFF, SON!

NEVER GIV UP, NEVER EVER GIVE UP...
EVENTUALLY WOMEN STOP BEING CRAZY,
FOR MOMENTS ANYWAY...BUT AS HARD AS
WE TRY, WE'RE STUPID, MOST OF THE TIME.

THE MAINS

The Best Pan Seared Ribeye STEAK She Ever Had...

Lucca's TAGLIATELLE with Roma SAUCE

Wild MUSHROOM QUINOA
With Braised Baby BOK CHOI

Whole steamed Red SNAPPER
with Sizzling PEANUT oil and CILANTRO

SALMON 101 – Perfectly Seared Salmon Filet

MOM's Fried CHICKEN

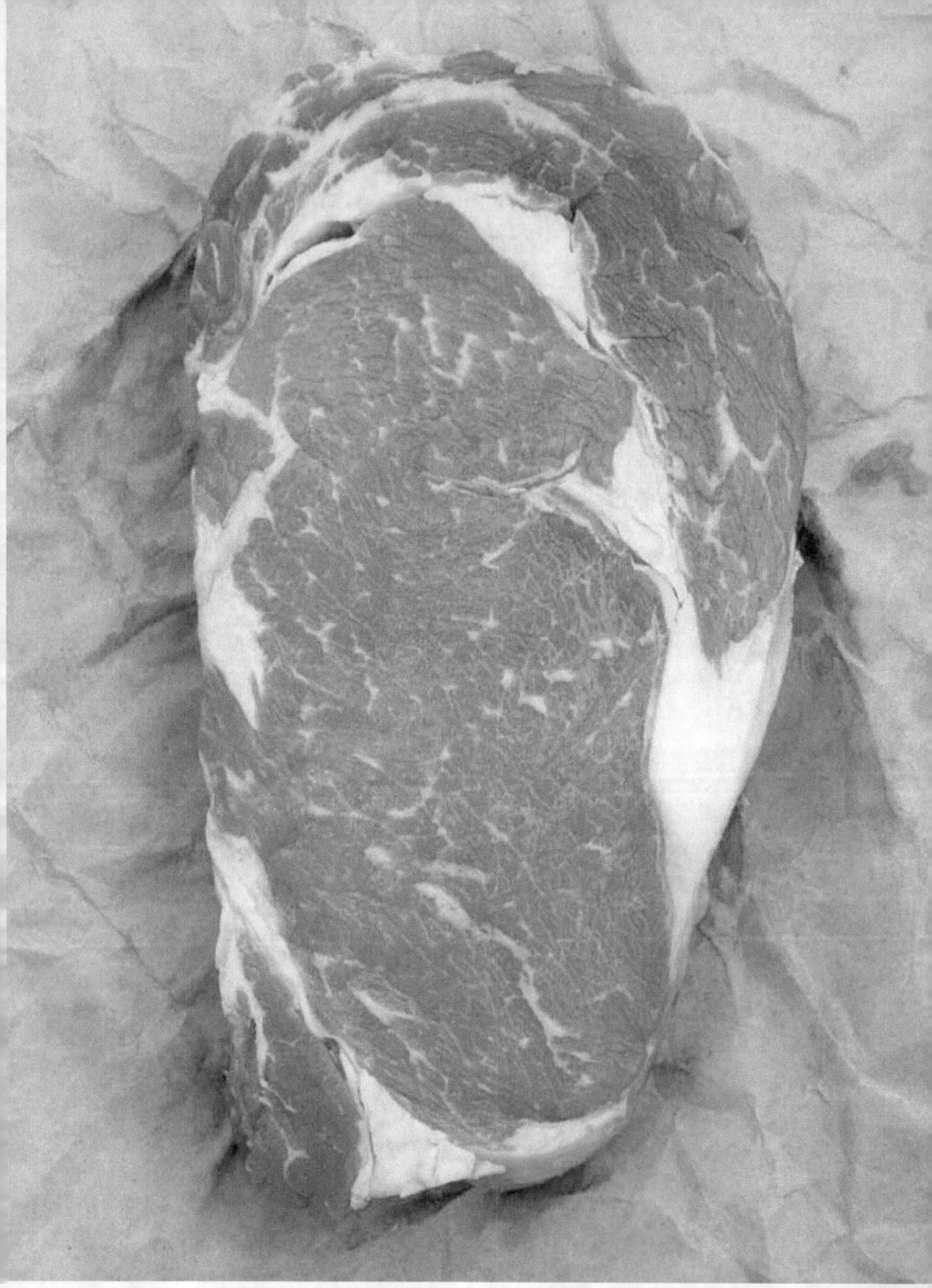

The Best Pan Seared Ribeye STEAK, SHE Ever Had

The star of this dish is, of course, the meat. The right pan, the co-star. You are the DIRECTOR, **an overcooked piece of meat is like a Sports Illustrated Swimsuit Model with a** BIG BUSH, **it's a** TRAVESTY!

INGREDIENTS

A "Good" Saute Pan
2in PRIME Ribeye Steak
> The BUTT is the best part, will explain later...

Extra Virgin Olive Oil Canola/vegetable oil
Truffle Oil
> (optional, only because it's a lil' pricey and you might be a **lotta' cheap**. But it does make a HUGE difference.)

Sea salt and fresh ground pepper

DIRECTIONS

It is crucial your MEAT be at room temp before cooking. This will make for even, perfect cooking. So let it be on your counter for at least 115-20 mins beforehand.

LIBERALLY season YOUR MEAT with sea salt, fresh ground pepper, and a nice slather of olive oil 10 mins before cooking. Preheat oven at 400.

If you don't have an "oven-safe" pan, meaning no part of it is plastic or rubber, place a glass baking dish in the oven as it heats.

When the time has come and *your meat is "warmed up"*, heat your pan on high heat with a "1 count" of canola or veggie oil.

Your pan is ready when you see A HINT of smoke, try to coat your pan evenly with the oil that is now hot.

Carefully place your steak in the pan.

There will be smoke, let it **BE**

A nice sear comes from high, HIGH HEAT.

Like bacon, (again using this analogy because it is something you can understand...)

we want a nice caramel brown crust on your steak.

And let me repeat, this comes from HOT, hot hEAT.

Keep it at high and be patient not screwing with your meat,

let it be brown...3 minutes for a nice crust.

Flip and sear the other side for 3 minutes, ONLY. Wait for the CRUST...!

Please remember, these cooking times and temps apply to at the very least,

1½ - 2in thick piece of meat, **the THICKER the better.**

So don't be cheap and screw up my recipe...!

Now, with the perfect sear on both sides, finish in oven.

Again, if the pan is oven "safe" throw the whole lot of it in the oven.

If not...remove from pan and place your piece of meat in the glass dish that is waiting

for you in the oven. Finish in oven for 4 minutes.

Remove your PAN/glass dish from oven and let YO' **MEAT** rest on a plate or cutting board for at least

5 minutes. Remember, your meat will continue to cook as it rests,

retaining all of its juices.

Finish your **beautiful piece of meat** with a nice drizzle of truffle or olive oil and

a lil' pinch of sea salt.

As for the BUTT, it's the "collar" of the ribeye.

No matter how your steak is done,

if it is off one way or the other (DO NOT let this happen!)

Under or overcooked, **the butt will always taste perfect.**

And this should be the first bite she takes. Take a slice of the butt and offer it to her,

Oh, meaty heaven...

Remember, it's all about the meat.

The **taste of good meat, perfectly cooked is unforgettable-**

Tender, the perfect shade of PINK, juicy, oh so juicy,

Saltiness that **FEELS** right in HER MOUTH,

Let your meat **speak for itself...!**

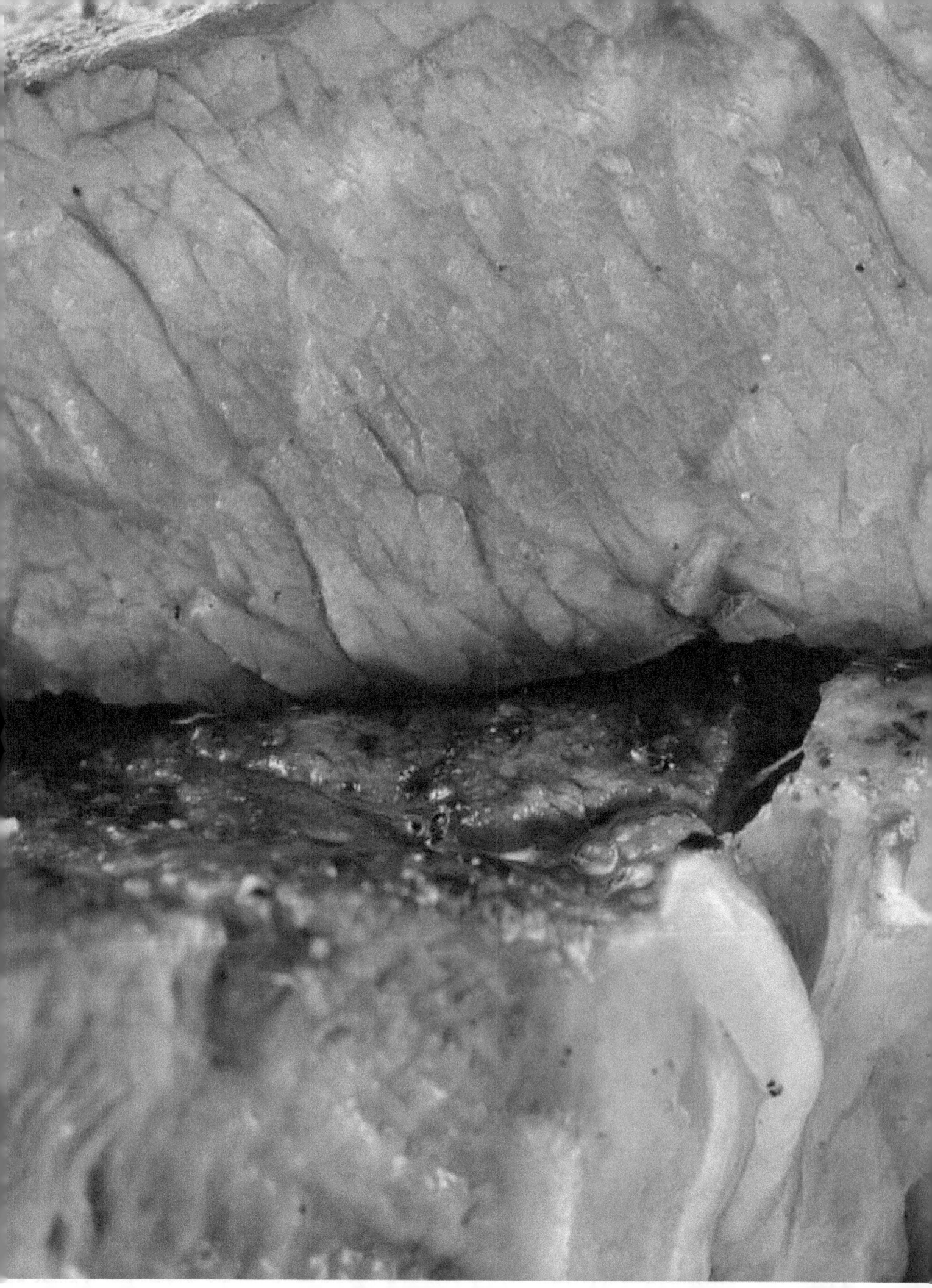

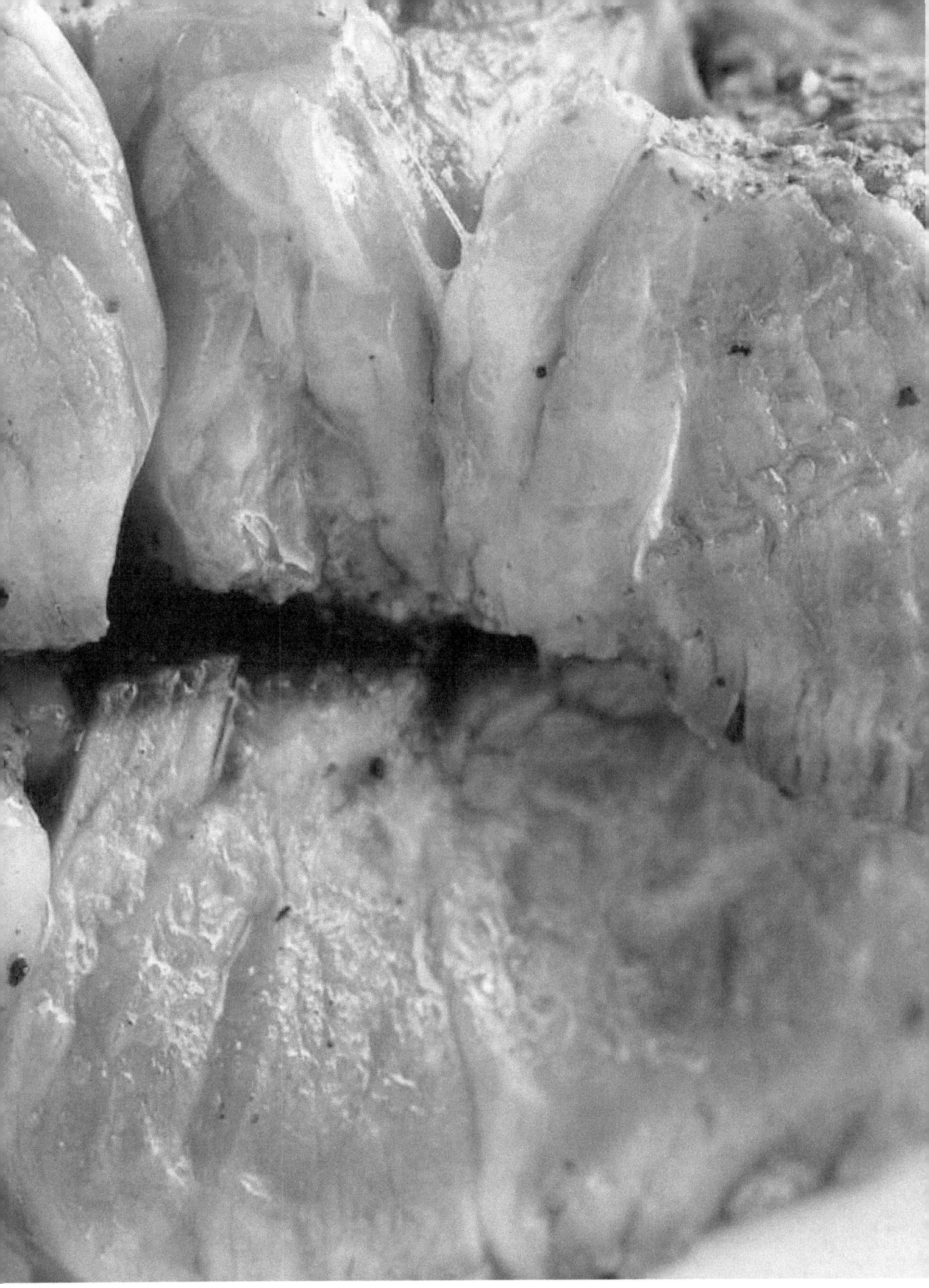

Lucca's Tagliatelle with Roma SAUCE

Lucca is from ROME, he's ITALIAN, he's a hairstylist, **he gets** B.I.T.c.h.e.s and he makes damn good sauce!

INGREDIENTS

1lb. dry Tagliatelle or Fettuccine
  (tagliatelle just sounds better...)
1 full rack Baby Back Ribs
3 Spicy Italian Sausages
1/4 lb. Premium ground Beef
6 Roma tomatoes
8 Cloves fresh Garlic
The Holy Trinity
  1 medium White Onion
  4 stalks of cleaned Celery
  4 Carrots, cleaned but not skinned
Red Chili Flakes
1 28oz canned Vine Ripened chopped
  tomatoes
1 24oz jar of Pasta Sauce
  NOT Ragu! most anything that costs more than $6 will be decent. Chose something that sings to your senses, a taste you've been curious about and wanting to try.
Drinkable Red Wine
Fresh Parmesan Cheese
Extra Virgin Olive Oil
Sea salt and fresh ground pepper

DIRECTIONS

There's a lot of ingredients and it sounds complicated but all you have to do is get it all in the pot and you're golden...

When dealing with any protein and vegetables at the same time, it's always smart to start with the veg first. Heat a "3 count" of olive oil in a LARGE sauce pot on high heat. You have a lot of veg, so remember the "CUT"...

Mire poix, pronounced "meer pwaa" is French for the trio of onion, celery, carrot. Dice and add your "meer pwaa" to the pot and brown. Smash and mince your garlic cloves and add to the mix. Roughly chop 6 ripe and plump roma tomatoes and set aside.

Now your **MEAT**...

If you bought real sausage, they come in their natural casing. if they didn't, you chose wrong...

With your kitchen sears, cut through the casing of each sausage, **eXposing the sausage goodness** inside. Add the **sausage goodness** to your pot and let it brown with all the other goodies, give it a nice stir and hit it with a "6 count" of olive oil.

Yo' BABY BACKS

To make it easier to work within your pot, section your rack into 3 or 4 equal parts, add to pot. At this point, there is definitely a lot going on. Try to work it so that the sausage and the ribs are GETTING GOOD HEAT, get that caramel brown going...

Add 1 cup of the **fabulous red wine** that you bought, uncap that pricey jar of tomato sauce add it to the mix. Season with a nice pinch or 2 of chili flake, 2 generous pinches of salt and 4 good turns of pepper. Give it all a nice stir, half cover your pot and simmer on medium for at least 1 hr 30 mins – 2 hours or **til' the meat is falling off DEM BONES.**

This is a good time to heat your pasta water, hopefully you have another large pot. Heat 3 to 4 quarts OR 2/3 full with water. Bring to a boil and add a "2 count" of olive oil and 2 generous pinches of salt.

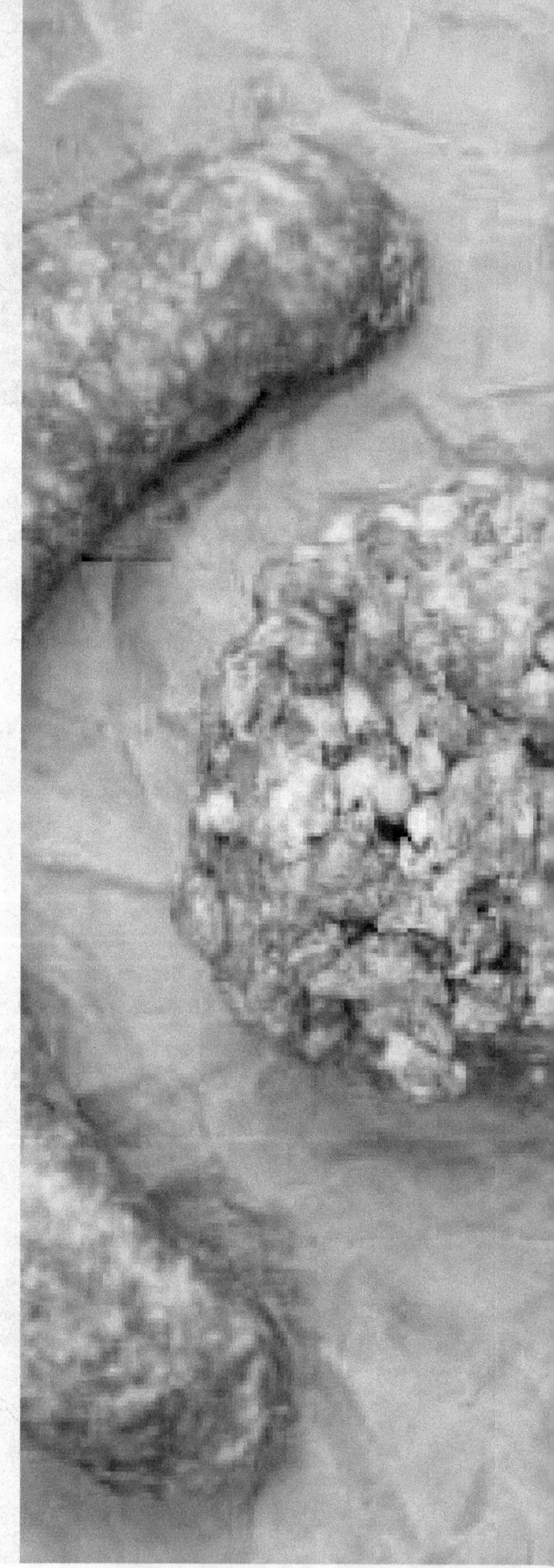

30 minutes before serving, add your fresh tomatoes to the sauce. TASTE YOUR SAUCE, and see if it needs anything- salt, some heat, maybe some sweetness...**add YOUR flavor**!

After 2 hours your sauce should be ready, you should have an easy time stripping the meat from the bones with a knife. Why did you do this with the bones? Because **bones add flavor-** bonehead!

Drop your pasta into your boiling water and get ready, it's almost done...One word here- "AL DENTE"! Italian for "firm to the tooth..." Or for you- **firm but NOt SOFT in the mouth.** All it means is, don't overcook your pasta! 8-12 minutes will suffice. Always good to give the pasta a nice stir, to avoid any clumping. Strain pasta and plate.

Top with very generous spoonfuls of your succulent sauce and garnish with freshly **shaved** parmesan. A hit of olive oil is also a **thing of** beauty...

Well, there you have it...
BELLISIMA FOR YOUR BELLA!
And it will taste even better tomorrow...

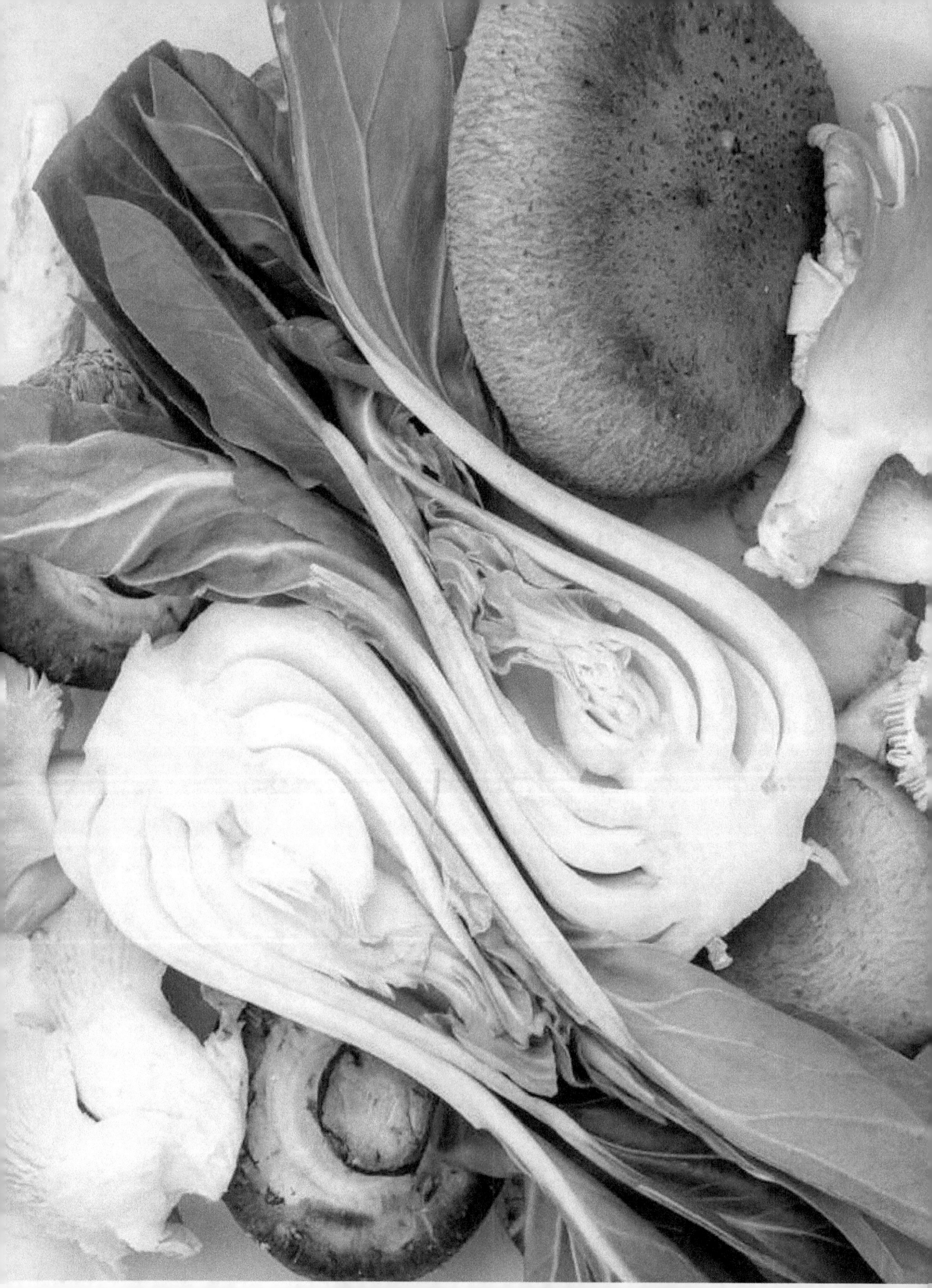

Wild Mushroom Quinoa
WITH BRAISED BABY BOK CHOI

Just in case she's a vegan/veg-head...and it's pronounced "keen-WA", and it's also from Peru.

INGREDIENTS

2 cups Quinoa
Wild Mushrooms
    handful of Shitake, Oyster and
    Portabello is a nice mix
3 stalks Baby Bok Choi
1 small White Onion
4 cloves Fresh Garlic
4 cups, Chicken Broth
Drinkable White Wine
Extra Virgin Olive Oil
A lil' Butter
Sea salt and fresh ground pepper

DIRECTIONS

Washing the QUINOA

With the 2 cups of quinoa in a medium sauce pan, give it a bath. Wash, **massage**, rinse and drain; trying hard not to lose any quinoa as you drain the water from the pot.

Place the sauce pan of rinsed and drained quinoa on high heat. Add smashed minced garlic and diced onion, sauté until that nice "carameling" starts to happen in the bottom of your pan. Add 4 cups CHICken broth to your sauce pan and bring to boil. At boil, reduce to medium heat cover and simmer on low heat.

YOUr MUSH…

If you got the time/patience- brush CLEAN each and every individual shroom. if not, then wash, rinse, drain and roughly chop your shrooms. Let the "Top Chefs" balk…

Heat your sauté pan on high heat with a "2 count" of olive oil, add sliced shrooms' and sauté til' "al dente", to re**fresh**: firm to the tooth but not soft...

Slice each of the 3 bok choi's in half and set aside.

With heat still on high, splash your shrooms' with "2 shots" of white wine, along with a 1/4 stick of butter. Add halved bok choi, cover and reduce heat to medium. Let simmer for 5 minutes then turn off heat, keeping lid on.

After 20-25 minutes your quinoa will be done, add a "2 count" of olive oil, A nice pinch of salt and 2 turns of the pepper grinder. Pop the lid off your baby boks, remember- cooked not limp.

With a wooden spoon or spatula give your quinoa a good mixing, creating a light, fluffiness.

Serving should be as such; a nice MOUND of quinoa, shrooms' scattered about the mound and the 3 halves of bok choi resting "**abstractly**" upon the MOUND.

Spoon some of the broth created by your shrooms' about the dish and give it one last splash of olive oil or if you have some truffle oil on hand, oooh yeah...!

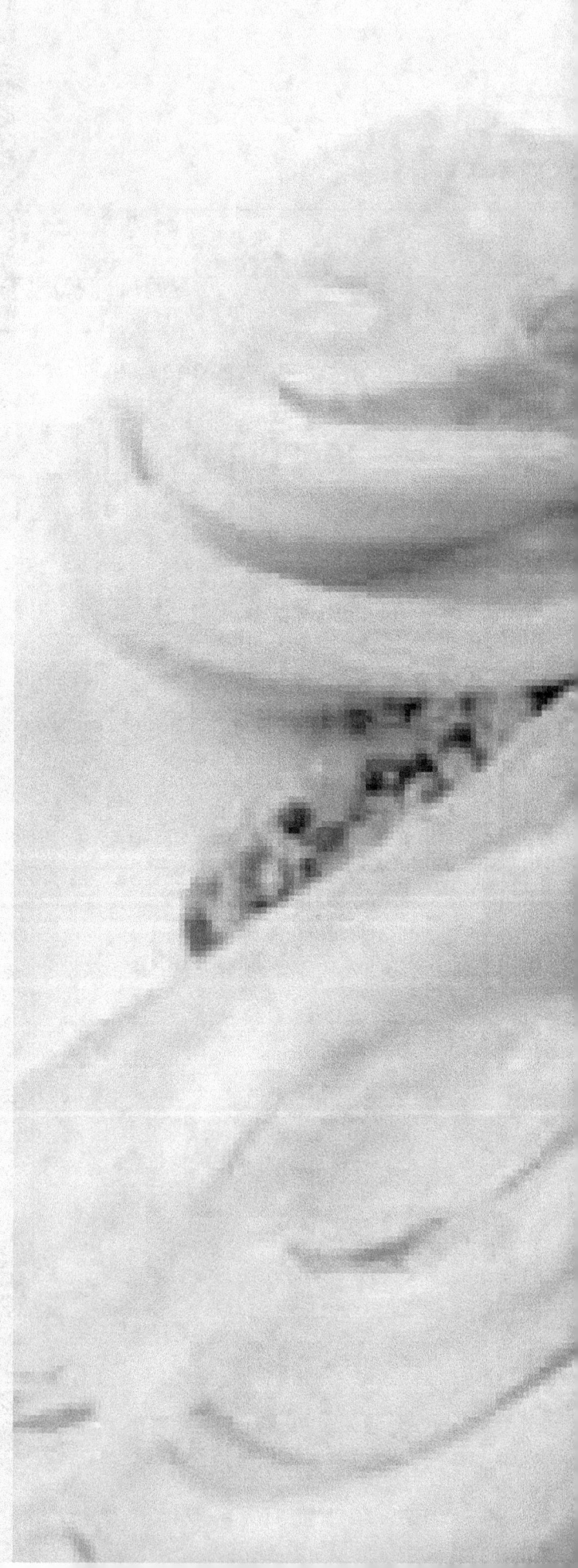

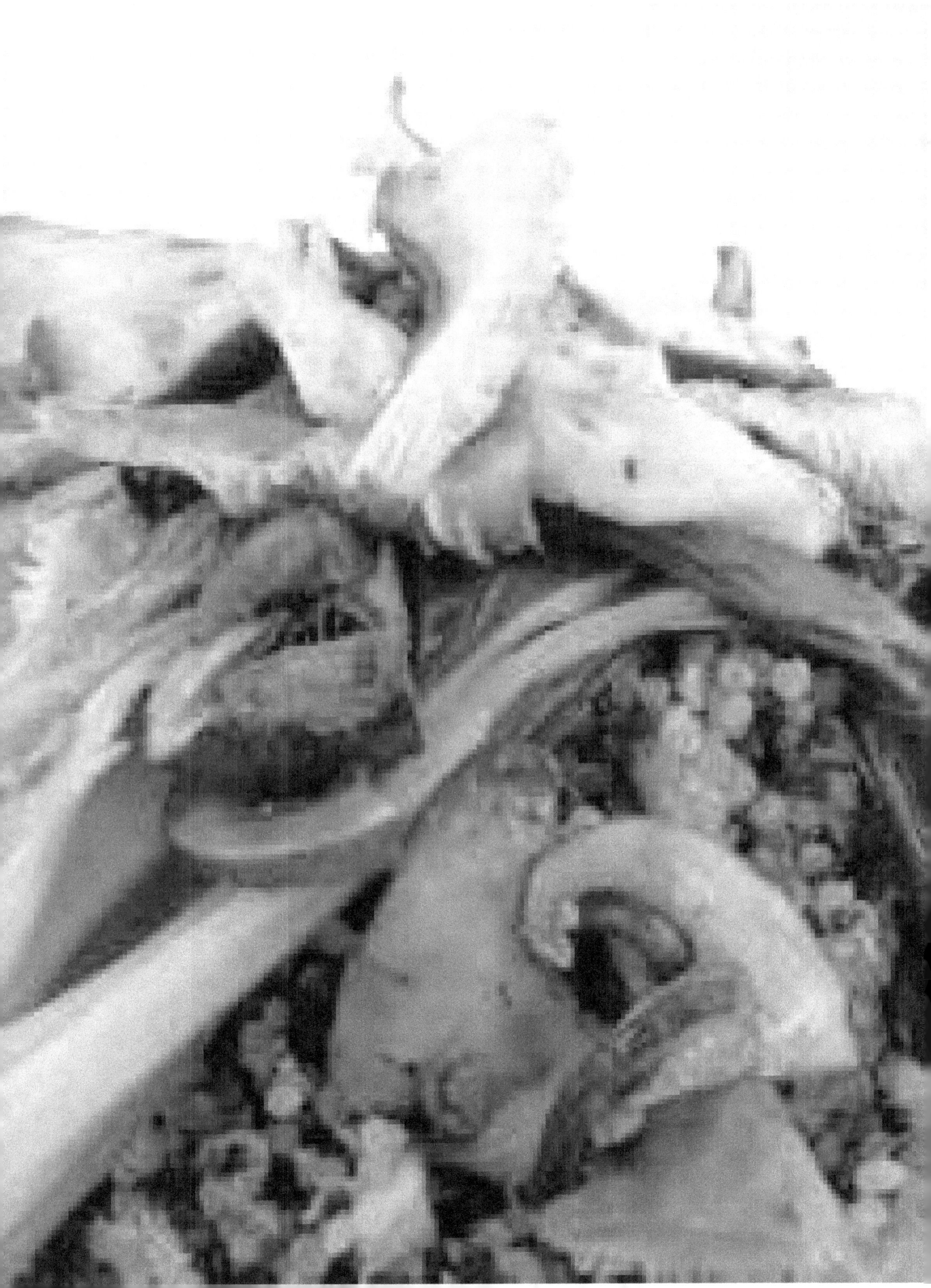

Whole steamed Red Snapper with
SIZZLING PEANUT AND CILANTRO

"Whole" includes the HEAD. Some people don't like their food looking back at them, if you must- you'll only LOOK LIKE a gentleman by taking the head off at the table...

INGREDIENTS

2lbs Fresh Whole Red Snapper
    scaled and gutted
2 bunches Cilantro
1 bunch Green Onion
Soy Sauce
Peanut Oil Sea salt and fresh ground pepper
Aluminum Foil
Ice Cubes

DIRECTIONS

Preheat oven at 450.

In a medium sauce pan, warm at medium heat, 12oz of peanut oil. This usually amounts to 3/4 the standard bottle sold in stores.

Set aside 6 sheets of aluminum foil of equal size, that are at least 6 inches longer than your fish. Place the 1st sheet of foil on your working surface (counter top or cutting board) and place your SCALED, GUTTED, FRESH whole snapper on the sheet of foil. Pat dry your fish with paper towel getting rid of any excess moisture. Season liberally with salt and pepper- inside and out.

"Strategically" place 8 ice cubes on top of your snapper in line running down the length of his body, Huh?! Just DO IT!! Keeping the cubes in place, take your 2nd sheet of foil and cover your fish,

Sealing the edges tight, like a nicely rolled FATTY-

So nothing can Get IN and nothing can get OUT.

Ok, because you're wondering...to steam you need moisture, **liquid**. Once heated, the ice melts, creating steam in your homemade foil pressure cooker. (**Holy**, CRAP...!)

Finish wrapping and sealing your snapper with the remaining 4 sheets of foil.

Watch yourself and the fish, the foil must stay intact, **NO** Holes!

Softly lay your snapper in the oven on a cooking sheet and cook for 20 minutes.

For anything bigger, add 6 minutes per pound.

WASH your 2 bunches of cilantro. Pat dry any excess moisture and with **your brute strength**, separate the leaves from the stalks with one quick twist.

Cut the green onion stalks in half, then split each stalk down the middle.

For presentation and for the sake of cleanliness, ready your 9x13 baking dish

Turn up the heat on your oil to high, TIME TO SIZZLE...

Remove foiled fish from oven and place in glass dish, still not breaking the seal.

Remember, your fish will continue to cook if kept sealed. So, don't keep him or her waiting.

Alright, the "Big show" with the snapper is with the oil. When you and your special someone are ready, carefully slice open the foil- kitchen shears are always easy. With the steam rising and **the whole fish swimming in its' wonderful broth looking back at you**, splash your snapper with a "6 count" of soy sauce and "dress" him with your

Cilantro leaves and green onion slices.

Now, with your friend at a SAFE distance but close enough so she can witness YOUR SKILLS, using a oven mitt or at least a towel, take your smoking hot peanut oil and slowly, NOt **dumping** or **dousing**, but carefully pour, drizzle it over your fish.

The **hot oil** will instantly, **sear** and SIZZle your cilantro and green onions, making for the "Big show".

Just do it, it'll be cool...

Peanut oil is light and healthy. And upon eating the most **succulent** and moist fish you or she ever had, you will find that it is NOT oily whatsoever...

Salmon 101 – Perfectly Pan Seared Salmon Filet

So simple, so good...But as with a fine steak, so is the same with this pink fish- OVERcOOKEd is a travesty like a BIG bush!

INGREDIENTS

A "Good" Saute Pan
Fresh Salmon filet with skin
Standard is usually a 6oz filet
Sea salt and fresh ground pepper
Extra virgin Olive Oil

DIRECTIONS

Heat your pan on high heat with a "1 count" of olive oil. Your pan is ready when you see A HiNT of smoke, try to coat your pan evenly with the oil that is now hot. Give your filet a 3 finger pinch of salt and 2 turns of pepper. Carefully place your filet in the pan skin side up. There's gonna be smoke, there's gonna be smells so turn on the fan and open the windows. Searing at high heat seals flavor and moisture in, so deal with it... 3-5mins will give you that perfect crust, turn your fish and lower your heat just a tad. Cover it with your lid from your sauce pan and finish searing for another 3mins. This will cook your fish evenly, from top to bottom.

Remember, once out of the pan, your fish will continue cooking. So don't let it sit too long before eating. And it SHOULD be PINK, "**medium**" on the inside.

If you're worried about gettin' sick and you serve it well done, you need to GROW A SET and YOU'RE SHAMEFUL! you might as well open a can of salmon and throw it in front of her.

PINK IS GOOD AND TASTY!

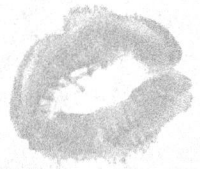

MOM's Fried Chicken

My MOM was the **most amazing woman** I have ever known and her chicken was pretty damn good...!

INGREDIENTS

Drumsticks
    Usually the best, not too big...
    10 is a good number of legs
Array of Spices
Poultry Seasoning, 4 tbsp
Paprika, 2 tbsp
Cayenne Pepper, 1 tbsp
Ancho Chili Powder, 1 tbsp
Sea salt, 4 generous pinches
Fresh ground pepper, 8 turns
Sifted All Purpose Flour, 3 cups
Eggs, 3
Peanut Oil
Safflower Oil

DIRECTIONS

In a medium saucepan, heat 3 cups peanut oil and 1 cup safflower or vegetable oil over medium-high heat. Allow at least 15 minutes to heat. Preheat oven to "Warm" temp.

In your good ole' 9x13 baking dish, sift together flour, spices, salt, and pepper. use your fingers, meshing spice and flour, making sure every bit of flour is flavored. Give it a taste, **you're the "chef".** If you feel it needs "something", take care of IT Emeril, and make it better...Crack 3 whole eggs in a separate large bowl and beat!

Each leg goes into your spiced flour, egg, then flour again. Completely cover the suckas...!
Flour-egg-flour-
That's how it goes Johnny...

The **long**er your legs sit in the spiced flour before going into the fryer, the MORE FLAVOR they will have.

As oil is heating, batter your first **set of legs**. Once the first set goes into the oil, batter the second set and so forth, and so on...

Drumsticks take up to 14 minutes to cook, 7 minutes per side. You want a golden, crisp brown so adjust your heat accordingly. Medium high is a good place to start.

Ready a brown paper bag and lay it flat on a cooking sheet. When your drumsticks are finished cooking, place them on the paper bag lined baking sheet (to sop up excess oil) and place them in the oven to keep warm.

Once all drumsticks are cooked and warming in the oven, they are

GOOD TO EAT AT ANYTIME.

Your legs are good **hot, warm, cold**. They're also pretty damn good out of the fridge the next morning...

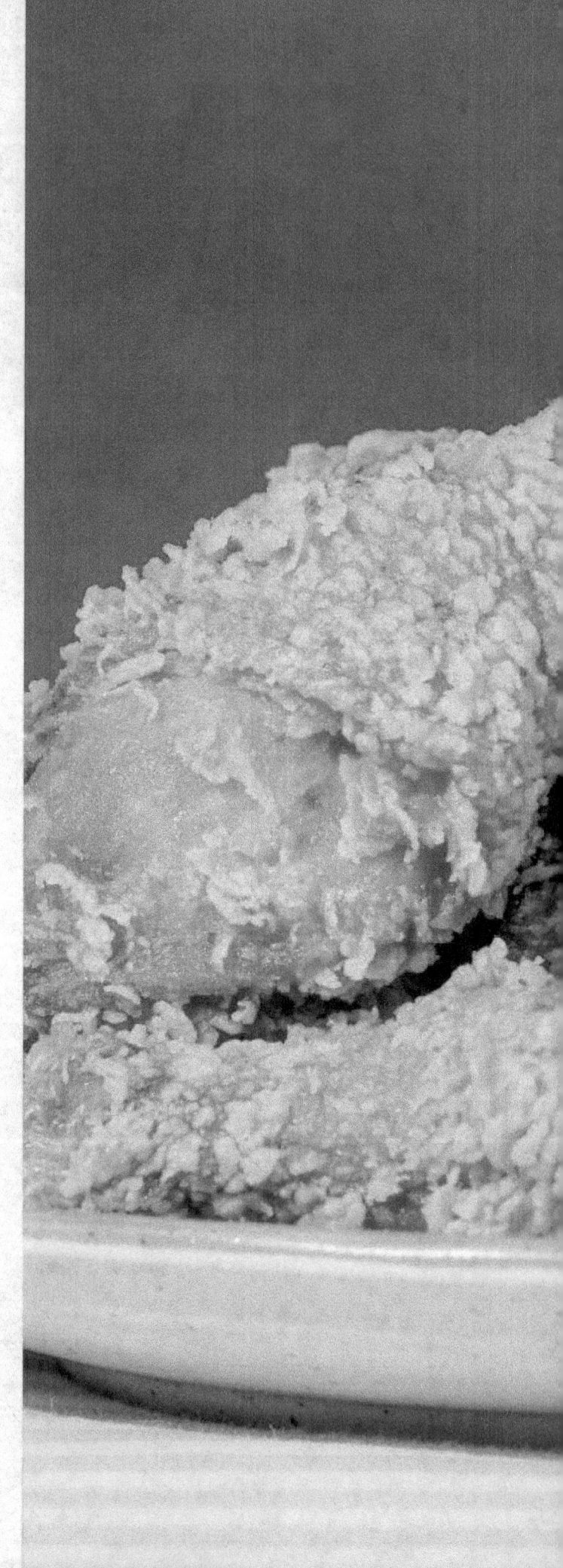

YOU'RE DONE COOKIN BITCH!

GIVING IN, DOESN'T MEN GIVING UP...IN THE END, WOMEN ARE STILL CRAZY BUT WE LOVE THEM AND THAT'S THE ONE THING MAKES US SMART, IF ONLY FOR A BRIED MOMENT...

DESSERT
Gourmet Chocolate
Italian Gelato

DIRECTIONS
Wholefoods,
$20,
2 pints of **Italian** GELATO,
3 **bar**s of chocolate...!

LIFE IS A, B.I.T.C.H ...!

LIFE is BEAUTIFUL, INTENSE, TENDER, COMPLICATED, HEAVENLY ...

MAY YOU CHOOSE TO SEE IT, TASTE IT, TOUCH IT, LISTEN TO IT AND FEEL IT DEEP DOWN IN YOUR SOUL EVERYDAY OF YOUR LIFE. MAY YOUR WINE BE BOLD AND YOUR STEAKS THICK AND JUICY. BUT MOST OF ALL — MAY YOUR SUNRISES AND SUNSETS AND ALL THE MOMENTS IN BETWEEN BE SHARED WITH THE ONE YOU LIKE, LOVE AND CRAVE.

Le MENUs

SO, I leave it **up to you** and your tastes to fashion a meal- an eXperience-
To creating an amazing evening for you and a friend.

Suggestions not directions
1) Give me a steak and a bottle of Cab and I'm happy.
And most **women who love meat** as much as I do will agree.
2) Pistachios go with everything.
May it be the starter to the starter or the finisher to the dessert,
Nuts **are always good to have around.**

But alas...

Nuts, Cutting Board, Romaine Salad, Steak, Brussels
Nuts, Cutting Board, Snapper
Nuts, Clams, Salmon, Quinoa
Nuts, Romaine, Salad, Pasta
Nuts, Poke, Steak,
Nuts, Chicken, Mac Salad
Nuts, Ceviche, Steak
Nuts, Romaine Salad, Chicken, Quinoa
Nuts, Ceviche, Steak, Quinoa
Nuts, Cutting Board, Pasta
Nuts, Ceviche, Poke, Snapper
Nuts, Romaine Salad, Steak and Snapper
Nuts, Poke, Chicken, Brussels
Nuts, Clams, Steak
Nuts, Pasta, Steak
Nuts, Ceviche, Poke, Cutting Board
Nuts, Salmon, Slaw
Nuts, Steak, Slaw
Nuts, Salmon, Brussels
Nuts, Slaw, Chicken
Nuts, Slaw Steak
Nuts, Slaw, Snapper

WHO the (h*ll) AM I!

For the past 10 years, I have spent over 15,000 hours working closely,
1 on 1, privately with women as their personal "half-priced therapist"/fitness trainer.
Listening to their **wants** and needs, hopes and dreams, their **tears** and their fears.
And I am very proud to say that,
ALL of them became, and most of them **to this day, are personal friends**.

I've travelled the globe extensively, experiencing the very best and most interesting food from countless
countries and cultures.
And I routinely cook for and partake in the GLUTTONOUS GOURMET
Cuisine of The South Bay Supper Club- Los Angeles's premier foodie crew.

And if nothing else;

I LOVE FOOD, I LOVE FOOD, I LOVE FOOD. AND I LOVE WINE, I LOVE WINE, I LOVE WINE. BUT MOST OF ALL, I LOVE WOMEN

BECAUSE THEY'RE ALL

B.I.T.C.H.E.S …!

WORKING::

We B.I.T.C.H.E.S. Are still hungry! The 2nd date...

I'm hungry, B.I.T.C.H.?!- What guys want

Good morning, B.I.T.C.H., the breakfast book

Dinner OUT- On the town with the B.I.T.C.H.

Fat B.I.T.C.H., dessert...

Drunk ass B.I.T.C.H.,the drinks...

FIT B.I.T.C.H., How to be a healthy B.I.T.C.H.

She may be your Wife, but she is still a B.I.T.C.H.-
      Rebooting the Booty for married couples

Divorced, She's ready to be a B.I.T.C.H. again...

MOM's can be a B.I.T.C.H., what teens should know...

We're ALL B.I.T.C.H.E.S., The APPROACH...

Gettin' B.I.T.C.H.E.S.- The workout video

Follow Feedin' B.I.T.C.H.E.S. on Facebook

Contact me at J@feedinbitches.com

CREDITS:

Authored by J. Laciste

Layout & Design- Eric Laciste and Jeff Peterson

Much MAHALO to all my B.I.T.C.H.E.S ...

Virginia,
Tata Ben,
'Chelle,
Junie Lane and Auntie C,
KK Marie and Slippery V.
D.I.
The PRIDE-
MUMA,
Freeda Bandita,
Riff, Crumbs and Baba.
Papa and Butterscotch.
Elvis and Swiss Army RON.
And for asking the question-
Kel-McC.

B. EAUTIFUL

I. NTELLIGENT

T. ENDER

C. OURAGEOUS

H. EAVENLY

E. ROTIC

S. TRONG

www.ingramcontent.com/pod-product-compliance
Lightning Source LLC
Chambersburg PA
CBHW081002140626
46546CB00018B/2980